WISHING FOR A SNOW DAY

GROWING UP IN MINNESOTA

Peg Meier

MINNESOTA HISTORICAL
SOCIETY PRESS

www.mhspress.org

The Minnesota Historical Society Press is a member of the Association of American University Presses.

Manufactured in the United States of America

10 9 8 7 6 5 4 3 2 1

∞ The paper used in this publication meets the minimum requirements of the American National Standard for Information Sciences—Permanence for Printed Library Materials, ANSI Z39.48–1984.

FRONTISPIECE: Babies in a Minneapolis Maternity Hospital, ca. 1925

International Standard Book Number
ISBN 13: 978-0-87351-640-2 (paper)
ISBN 10: 0-87351-640-0 (paper)

LIBRARY OF CONGRESS CATALOGING-IN-PUBLICATION DATA

Wishing for a snow day : growing up in Minnesota / [edited by] Peg Meier.
    p. cm.
Includes bibliographical references and index.
ISBN-13: 978-0-87351-640-2 (pbk. : alk. paper)
ISBN-10: 0-87351-640-0 (pbk. : alk. paper)
1. Children—Minnesota—Biography—Anecdotes. 2. Youth—Minnesota—Biography—Anecdotes. 3. Minnesota—Social life and customs—Sources. 4. Minnesota—Social life and customs—Pictorial works. 5. Minnesota—Biography—Anecdotes. I. Meier, Peg, 1946–
CT242.W57 2010
977.6'054092—dc22
[B]   2009015087

Contents

for REBECCA,
WHO BRINGS OUT
THE CHILD IN ME

Wishing for a Snow Day

Introduction

My great-niece Sara—and she is great—was a little past two years old when she invented a word that has become a family tradition. Christmas was coming, and Sara made it clear that she was way past plain-old excited. She kept saying, "I'm so sur-cited. I am just *soooo sur-cited.*"

Sur-cited is a word I have often used while exploring the lives of generations of Minnesota children. I've not only been excited; I've been surprised, too. Surprised by the intensity and intelligence of what children said and wrote; excited by elders' memories of childhood. Surprised by the vivid accounts of children's deaths and the depth of parents' grieving; excited by lovely stories of play and friends and good times.

Let me tell you about some of my favorites.

- A North Shore boy in 1935 wrote an essay about geese, beginning, "Geese is a low heavy-set bird which is mostly meat and feathers. His head sits on one side and he sits on the other."

- Sweet little June Oberg, age nine in Two Harbors in 1931, was so sad about a kindergarten friend whose relatives often whipped her that June wrote to the governor for help.

- A Moorhead couple commissioned a family portrait in about 1886. The man looks to be in shock. No wonder. The family had lost three children to scarlet fever in March 1885, *two in one day.*

- Coco Irvine, one of the state's richest children, grew up in the house on St. Paul's Summit Avenue that is now the Governor's Residence. She was almost thirteen years old when she wrote on the first day of 1927, "Dear Diary, This is to be my most private account of everything that happens to me . . . Everything is getting quite different in my life because of boys! I absolutely like one now. I guess he likes me too. This diary is to keep track of how things go. And so I can analyze the best way of making certain he likes me. He sure acts like he doesn't, which is a good sign."

For several years, I happily dug around in papers and photos at Minnesota historical societies and in private collections, looking for stories of children. Such a sense of discovery! Open a box at the Minnesota History Center and find a girl's journal of crossing the state in a covered wagon. Check the diary of a friend's great-grandfather and find a boy's perception of Civil War times. See reports of children who came from the East on "orphan trains" and were chosen by families at train depots, more for their muscles than for love.

It's been fun—actually, "sur-citing"—to see how childhood today is much as it was in the past and, of course, how different.

Margaret Jackson Bovey, who was born in 1887 and died in 1972, wrote in her memoir in the 1950s about those differences: "I have had it in the back of my mind for a long time to write a sketch of my childhood. It is not that my childhood was a particularly interesting one, for it wasn't, but I think people of my generation have lived in two entirely separate worlds, and I want to put down for my children as much as I can remember of that comparatively simple, easy, pleasant and, what seems to us now, primitive way of life, in contrast to the present time so unsettled, so full of change and insecurity."

Could it be that many of us who are well into adulthood now think that we too have lived in two entirely separate worlds?

For most of human history, childhood has been anything but easy. In medieval times, it is estimated that one or two of three infants died. Sociologists formerly speculated that early deaths caused families to refrain from getting attached to young children. (More recent scholarship disputes this view: the birth of almost every child was hoped for, benefiting both family and the larger society.) When depicted in art—and that wasn't until the twelfth century—children looked like adults, but in smaller scale. Early Puritans in America called a child "it" until weaned. As late as the 1800s, when a young child died, parents would use the same name for the next infant.

For most of human time, a child older than five to seven was absorbed into the world of adults. Most children were expected to work, to contribute to the family's upkeep, to help raise younger siblings. Childhood was brief.

Recorded history in Minnesota is relatively short; we can't document the profound changes here since medieval times. Some of the earliest entries are from the 1830s. It was then that Catherine Ely kept a journal of raising her first child, Mary. Catherine, whose ancestry was part Ojibwe, and her husband, Edmund, served as missionaries to the Indians in northern Minnesota. She recorded that their baby sought attention but her husband fretted that the child would become spoiled. Parents squabble about similar topics today, although few now would note, as Catherine did in the baby book, that a seven-month-old liked sucking on rabbit bones.

The earliest guidebooks encouraging immigration to Minnesota rarely mentioned children, though. Most in the 1860s and 1870s made a quick note that there were schools. That's it. Writers saw no need to appeal to children's interests. Where parents went, children went.

For generations, Minnesota children labored in mills, on farms, in homes. Sociologists say that only since World War II have a majority of American children been educated, well cared for, and free from adult responsibilities.

I don't pretend that what I found for this book is representative of most Minnesota children's lives. People who are likely to think their stories are significant enough to be preserved are middle and upper class, white, educated, and happy about their young lives. I think of the exuberant ten-year-old Glanville Smith of St. Cloud writing in his diary about a picnic: "I sure no we sertenly had a good time of it, all righty!"

However, juvenile thugs, misfits, and unloved children didn't leave records of their misdeeds and miseries. Adults recorded some of them—in court records, in newspapers, in letters. I've included samples of those stories too, to diminish the lore of the supposed "good old days." Childhood has always been a mixed bag.

To further complicate the picture, memory plays tricks, especially recollections of the distant past. Pleasant memories expand with age, and they're the ones we savor. We save proof of childhood happiness—loving letters and photos, comforting teddy bears, crayon drawings, raggedy books—maybe for the next generation, maybe just for ourselves. Our brains continue to dredge up old nursery rhymes, songs, and hymns, played back at the oddest times. We tell childhood stories that make people chuckle, and we share even some of the weepy tales that somehow make us feel good for the telling.

At least that's true for those of us with the great good fortune of having wonderful childhoods. Born nine months and three days after my parents celebrated the end of World War II on V-J Day, I was unplanned and cherished. I was a blissful kid (some would say spoiled), and that makes me happy to this day.

Because I didn't have children of my own, I've had to glom onto other people's kids. Thanks to my family and friends for allowing me that joy.

Biographies

Here are some of the Minnesotans who wrote accounts of their childhoods, pieces of which are reprinted on these pages.

Frederick Allis. 1848–1921. Born in New Orleans, he moved with his family to St. Paul in 1856 as his father sought a healthier climate. Fred, a fine student, started keeping a diary at age fifteen and went on to graduate from Yale University and Columbia Law School.

William Bircher. 1845–1917. After the Civil War, William and his father both returned safely to West St. Paul. He married, had three children, and ran a popular saloon called Billy Bircher's Place in West St. Paul.

Lena L. Borchardt. 1892–1972. Born Lena Louise Goldeman, she recorded her memories of her Swiss grandparents, her family's life in north Minneapolis from the 1890s to 1906, and later life on a small farm just north of the city. Her father worked in the flour mills. She and her husband, Arthur Borchardt, farmed near Willow River and joined the Communist Party in 1936.

Margaret Jackson Bovey. 1887–1972. In a reminiscence written for her descendants in the 1950s, Margaret, the daughter of a lawyer, included stories about her family life in Minneapolis in the 1890s.

Ruth F. Brin. 1921–2009. Both Ruth and her mother graduated from Vassar College. Ruth became an accomplished poet and wrote a published memoir called *Bittersweet Berries: Growing Up Jewish in Minnesota*.

Polly Bullard. 1881–1949. Polly and her sister Marjorie grew up in St. Paul. Polly kept diaries of school life and social activities, and as an adult she recorded her "Reminiscences of Things Past." Polly went on to live on the Mesabi iron range and to teach school in Eveleth.

Anna Lathrop Clary. 1859–? She grew up in the little frontier town of Anoka, the daughter of a Methodist minister. Her children asked her to write the stories of her early life, resulting in her 1939 published reminiscence.

William M. Cummings. 1917–95. His family moved from Kansas City, Missouri, to Redwood Falls in 1919 and to St. Paul in 1923. In a diary he kept in distinguished handwriting beginning at age fifteen, he related his dislike of school and his habitual truancy. William dropped out of high school and maintained a lifelong interest in book collecting and bird watching. He and his wife had five children. In 1957 the family moved to Berkeley, California, where he was an animal caretaker and school custodian.

Maria Rice Dawson. 1865–1957. One of eleven children of Edmund Rice, an early mayor of St. Paul and a U.S. senator, she grew up at Trout Brook, the Rice family's country home in what was then St. Paul, now Minneapolis. She married William Dawson, whose father succeeded Rice as St. Paul mayor.

Iva Andrus Dingwall. 1877–? Iva's remembrances include stories of her youth near Elk River, especially about attending country dances with her fiddler father. She went on to play the violin herself and to teach music for many years in Superior, Wisconsin. Recordings of her fiddle music are in the Minnesota Historical Society collections.

W. E. B. DuBois. 1868–1963. He spent an unpleasant summer in 1888 with other black youths as waiters at a fancy Lake Minnetonka hotel. He became a prominent civil rights activist and author.

Charles Eastman, or Ohiyesa ("The Winner"). 1858–1939. The son of a Dakota father and half-white mother, he was sent to a mission school in the early 1870s. His first day there, he was jeered by other pupils and fled. He reluctantly returned to the classroom. Seventeen years later, he graduated from Boston Medical College, one of the first American Indian physicians and an outstanding athlete. He wrote of his youthful years in his 1902 book, *Indian Boyhood.* His grandfather was the celebrated painter Seth Eastman.

Gerhard A. Ellestad. 1898–1986. He grew up in Lanesboro and graduated from St. Olaf College and George Washington University Law School. He worked on the East Coast until 1959, when he and his wife returned to Northfield, where he practiced patent law. He published his memoir, *Small-Town Stuff,* in 1985.

Evelyn Fairbanks. 1928–2001. Born out of wedlock, she was raised by loving relatives. In 1990 she wrote a warm reminiscence, *Days of Rondo,* about St. Paul's thriving black community in the 1930s and 1940s. In the Twin Cities, she worked many jobs, including in a factory, as director of a neighborhood arts center, and as cashier at Hamline University, where she was the first black employee and which later awarded her an honorary doctorate. In retirement, near Onamia she ran a twenty-acre tree farm, which she said was more like a tree museum because she rarely cut down trees.

Clotilde "Coco" Irvine. 1914–75. Daughter of the St. Paul lumberman Horace Hills Irvine, she was born in what's now the Governor's Residence. She and her sister, Olivia Irvine Dodge, donated the 16,000-square-foot home to the state in 1965. Coco kept a hilarious diary of her life in 1927, when she turned thirteen years old. Her sister had it privately published in 1975 for family Christmas gifts, but Coco, by then known as Coco Churchill Moles, died before the holiday.

Sandra Kreamer. 1943– . Six months after her birth, her parents rented an apartment in "the projects" off Olson Memorial Drive in Minneapolis, which served mostly Jewish and black people who were denied housing in much of the Twin Cities. The family moved to north Minneapolis in a few years. Sandra raised three children, including a girl from Korea, and founded a group for Minnesota Jewish families with internationally adopted children. She lives in Minnetonka and Austin, Texas.

Irene Lindahl Krumpelmann. 1908–? She grew up in Duluth, Two Harbors, and Clear Lake, Wisconsin. Her first husband, Louis Iwanoski, ran a mortuary in St. Paul. He died in 1947. She was divorced from her second husband, Willis Krumpelmann, in 1963 and went back to school at the University of Minnesota to renew her teaching career. She served in Liberia with the Peace Corps and taught fourth and fifth grades in St. Paul Public Schools.

Charles A. Lindbergh. 1902–74. Yes, *that* Charles Lindbergh, the aviator, author, and explorer. He spent boyhood summers in Little Falls. When he was fourteen, he drove his father, who was running for U.S. Congress, on a campaign trip and kept a careful diary, including ways to conserve fuel, a practice that was useful for his 1927 trans-Atlantic flight.

Walter Stone Pardee. 1852–1925. He was born in New Haven, Connecticut, and moved to Minneapolis at age fourteen to join his family, who had come a few years earlier, and work on his father's farm in Ramsey County. The family later lived in Minneapolis. Walter graduated from the University of Minnesota with a degree in civil engineering and architecture and worked in the offices of famed architect L. S. Buffington. He and his wife had two sons and a daughter.

Alexander Ramsey. 1815–1903. Alexander was one of Minnesota's foremost early politicians—territorial governor, state governor, St. Paul mayor, and U.S. senator. His firstborn, a boy, died at age three. Only eighteen months later, another son died at nineteen months old. His daughter, Marion, survived to adulthood, married, and had four children. After her husband became ill, Marion Ramsey Furness raised her children in her parents' home. The Alexander Ramsey House in St. Paul is open for public tours.

Jo Lutz Rollins. 1896–1989. One of four daughters of a Methodist minister, she became a well-known watercolor artist, concentrating on landscapes, including scenes in Minnesota. She taught at the University of Minnesota.

J. C. "Buzz" Ryan. 1900–1992. He grew up in the Bemidji area, where his father was a sawmill operator. Buzz helped establish the Sullivan Lake Civilian Conservation Corps camp (Camp Charles) near Brimson in 1933 and served as the camp forester until it closed in 1941, one of the state's longest-running CCC camps. His career with the state forest service ran from 1922 to 1970. He was named district forester at the Cloquet Valley State Forest in 1929, a position he held till he retired.

Fannie S. Schanfield. 1916– . Her family moved from New York City to Minneapolis before Fannie was born. The summer of her eighth year, her mother called her in from play and asked her to sit and have coffee with her. Then her mother began telling family stories in Yiddish. The coffee klatch sessions lasted all summer. Fannie later regretted that she didn't remember all the stories, but those she did she included in her reminiscence, "Ma I Wrote It Down."

Blanche Stoddard Seely. 1876–1963. This south Minneapolis girl grew up to be a well-known actress at the turn of the twentieth century. She was a contemporary and friend of such theater greats as Ethel Barrymore, Margaret Anglin, Alla Nazimova, and Henry Miller. As an adult, she wrote her life story.

Lillian MacGregor Shaw. 1891–1990. A country schoolteacher until she married Robert C. Shaw, she moved to International Falls, where she wrote a newspaper column for ten years, ran a flower shop for twenty-five years, and was instrumental in establishing a junior college. She was ninety-six years old when her son, Robert MacGregor Shaw, interviewed her about her early years in Minnesota and North Dakota.

Betty Powell Skoog. 1932– . Of Irish and Ojibwe descent, she was born to a single mother sixty miles north of Ely in a two-room log cabin built by her grandfather and was raised in the traditional ways of her Ojibwe grandmother along the wilderness of the Minnesota-Ontario border. With Justine Kerfoot, she wrote a memoir, *A Life in Two Worlds.* She and her husband, Ken, divide their time between Silver Bay and Silver Springs, Florida.

Glanville Smith. 1901–87. His diary in 1911, when he was ten years old in St. Cloud, reveals a third grader of many interests, including the environment, seasons and weather, his garden, and nature in general. A lifelong bachelor, he was a designer for the Cold Spring Granite Company and an avid reader, writer, pianist, and composer.

Isabel Shephard Tryon Thibault. 1903–83. She spent girlhood summers at Lake Minnetonka, recalled in *My Island: Memories of a Childhood on Gale's Island,* published in 1978 by the Excelsior–Lake Minnetonka Historical Society. Her father, Charles Tryon, was an attorney, and her maternal grandfather, Harlow Gale, was influential in early real estate.

Charlotte Ouisconsin (an early way to spell "Wisconsin") **Clark Van Cleve.** 1819–1907. She was only a few weeks old when her parents came to the region to help establish the first U.S. military post, later called Fort Snelling. Charlotte's childhood was spent there and at other army posts. She married another army man, Horatio P. Van Cleve, and wrote an autobiography in 1888, *Three Score Years and Ten.*

A Little Taste

Children's letters and diaries tell so much, not only of young lives but also of the larger world. First: a sample of young Minnesotans' records of the good, the bad, the ugly, and the sweetness of life. Know what? Kids always have said— and written—the darnedest things.

When I was 6 years old, we were living in the little frontier town of Anoka. One day we heard great noise and a man came running down the street, shouting at the top of his voice. Everyone rushed to the window, and I heard words that I could never forget. The man was crying: "Lincoln is shot! Lincoln is shot!" I saw Pa grab his hat and rush out. He said to my mother, "I am going down town to hear more." My mother looked very sad. I didn't understand what it was all about, but I knew that some great tragic event had happened.

Anna Lathrop Clary, 1865

When a child died [in the 1870s], the father had to measure its length, how wide the little shoulders were, then, with what few tools he had, fashion a little coffin to fit, while the heart-broken mother bathed and combed her darling's hair for the last time. Then together they would lift, and place with loving care, the earthly remains of dear one into the little home-made casket. Love was the same in 1870 as it is today [written in 1939]. Yes, sometimes, we think, stronger.

There were no undertakers to do these sad necessities, no neighbors for miles, no telephones, and no money. Many a home in the early days was left childless from diphtheria. There were no general cemeteries. The dead were buried on a lot on the farm, but Jesus will not forget those little ones when He comes.

W. W. [Mr. Billy] Smith

One rainy afternoon when I was 9 and [my brother] Cholly was 5, we had exhausted all our ideas of entertaining ourselves and cast about for something interesting to do. We had a large box full of picture cards, given away in those days at the grocer's, the druggist's and at the little store across from our school where we bought rubber gum, candy bananas, ginger snaps

A happy girl dressed up in a fine winter outfit, complete with a velvet collar, walked through the concourse of the St. Paul Union Depot in about 1949. Do you suppose she's carrying her dad's bag and portfolio?

and dill pickles at recess. They were very pretty cards: pink and red roses, little kittens and woolly dogs. At the end of the sofa there was a large bare white plastered section of wall with no pictures, and we proceeded to tack up all the picture cards with little carpet tacks, creating a section about two feet square completely covered. We thought our handiwork a thing of true beauty and could scarcely wait for Mother to come home from a neighbor's home to show it to her. Alas! She failed to appreciate the charm of it, but there was nothing she could do until, the following spring, she wallpapered the parlor.

Blanche Stoddard Seely, 1880s

I created panic one Sunday by running off with [my sister] Marg just before naptime.

For I was a runaway. I was also a greedy little beastie with a constant hankering for a neighbor's cookie jar. (This just might explain how I became the family fatty in my teens.) Mother tried various punishments. Tying me to a bedpost was not a cure, but when she threatened to tie my mouth shut, I chose to give up my neighborhood raids. I did so love to talk!

But one Sunday afternoon at Breezy Point, the urge hit me again and I took Marg by the hand and set off along the shore to the Washburns. The hunt was long and anxious. When the family caught up with us, we were sitting very straight in the Washburns' living room, being treated as grown-ups. I expect we were given cookies . . .

The spanking that followed was one of Father's better ones. Big sister Betty took the other children back to the tennis court to get away from it all, but they did not escape. My stentorian bawls reached them easily.

Isabel Shephard Tryon Thibault, 1910s

Mar 21st 1911
I sure no we sertenly had a good time of it, all righty!

Glanville Smith

Coco Irvine, age thirteen, was precocious, scheming, and usually in trouble. Like the time she plotted to end lunches at her private school in St. Paul. As she liked to put it, "I am in grave trouble again through practically no fault of my own."

February 1st, 1927
Awful old school. At lunch we had codfish balls and old dead salad. I told Jeanie we could not go on this way and we must do something about our lunches or we would starve. She asked "What?" and I answered darkly, "I'll think of something."

February 3rd, 1927
I thought of something—but it ended in our getting suspended from all classes and not even being allowed to have recess or lunch hour. We were put in separate rooms for the whole day and they plan to have a meeting to discuss what to do with us. All this over practically nothing. All we did was wait til school was out yesterday. We hid in the cloakroom til everyone had left (we thought) and then we took all the knives and forks and spoons we could carry. (We put them in our pockets and in our bloomers and any place that would hold them.) We were planning to hide them, not steal them and sell them or anything like that. Only to hide them so we would have to go home for lunch until they could afford to buy new ones. It seemed like an innocent enough solution to the problem of how not to have to eat that awful food. Disastrously, as we were coming up the stone stairs, the rubber in Jeanie's bloomers broke and knives, forks and spoons were clattering down the stairs. I couldn't help but laugh only briefly for who should appear at the head of the stairs but Miss Holler. Words fail me. My despair was utterly complete. She of course saw no humor in the situation having no sense of

humor herself. She told us that she knew we were uncooperative but it never occurred to her we were thieves (Imagine) and that this was the worst deed which had ever transpired at Summit School and that our parents would be informed. Then she told us to go home after putting back every single knife, fork and spoon in its proper place. She stood grimly over us while this took place. Then gave us strict instructions to be in our seats at 8:30 the next day when Miss Converse (our principal) would deal with our punishment. She (Miss Holler) claimed she would not be surprised if we were expelled!

Thankfully mother and daddy are in the East.

February 5th

They had the meeting about us yesterday after school, and this morning Miss Converse told us we would not be expelled but would be suspended for one week. I argued that my marks were bad enough without missing a week of classes and she said, "You should have thought of that." Then for the rest of the term til Easter we cannot have recess or lunch period with the rest of the school, but must eat alone. Not even with each other. After school almost everyone in the class called me up. The majority feel a grave injustice has been done us. Some said they would have done the same thing had they thought of it. Jeanie and I feel it would have all been worthwhile if the lunches had improved. They didn't though, so we are martyred for nothing. Mother and daddy get home tomorrow—HELP!

February 6th

They got back this morning. I decided I better tell them all before anyone else did, so I met them at the door, crying. It was not all put on either as I was really scared nearly out of my mind. Daddy can be quite fierce and mother gets mad at much less things than this. Well, I worked myself into a good case of hysterics and cried so hard I couldn't talk. They got scared and probably thought I had found I had an incurable disease, or something. Daddy kept saying, "Come on now, nothing can be as bad as all that." Finally I decided they would probably forgive me anything they were so scared I would die of hysterics. They were very kind about it and decided I was being punished enough at school and I can even go to dancing school on Friday. It pays to know how to manage things. If I had been defiant, things might have had a disastrous turn for the worse. As it is, I feel so peaceful I can even enjoy being a martyr now. Daddy even said he didn't approve of children being kept from their classmates for so long a period. He may even talk to Miss Converse about it. I ate a huge breakfast. Nearly my first food since all this began. I don't even object to daddy thinking me a child. Sometimes I wish I were one. Life is simpler for them.

*　　*　　*

Herbert Dibley, age eight, was the winner of humorous declamation at the 1935 Minnesota State Fair. He looks to be a future debate star.

Intense ten-year-old Julia Schlianter won the lower-grade dramatic declamation at the same state fair. Her dress and hair ribbon were pressed and starched to the Nth degree.

An itinerant minister, whose last name was Johnson, often visited neighborhood homes, sharing Bible reading and prayer. One evening he stopped at our home as our parents [Fred and Minnie Samuelson] were going out to milk the cows. "The girls will have to entertain you until we're done with the chores," my mother told him. My older sister, Darlene, pondered how we should entertain him. Suddenly she remembered her poem book containing poems clipped from newspapers and magazines. Thumbing through its pages, she noticed a poem from the Prohibition era containing the name Johnson. "This poem's about you," she told the minister. "It even has your name in it."

She was a very adept reader, enunciating each word very distinctly. My younger sister, Stella, and I joined her, stumbling through it in unison: "Johnson, the drunkard, is dying tonight/With traces of sin on his face/He'll be missed at his place by the bar every night/Wanted—a boy in his place." Many verses in the same vein followed, and we read them all to him. Later we informed our mother how we had entertained him. She was horrified, almost to the extent of an anxiety attack!

Lydia Samuelson Simonson, 1930s

A letter from a child to Governor Floyd B. Olson:

Two Harbors, Minn.
March 19, 1931

Dear Mr. Olson,

I am a little girl 9 years old. I like school. I haven't been out [absent] one day. I like my techer very well. I feel pretty great to write to you.

This is June Oberg of Two Harbors at about age nine in 1931, when she took her concerns to the governor.

It is [about] a little girl that is in kindergarten she is adopted. If anyone says "Hello" she gets a wipping so some times she's on conshus [unconscious]. I don't know how to spell these big words just write. If she's cold she gets a wipping. When she's sick she has to lay on the cold floor. She hasn't any overshoes. She lives far from school. people have asked the ones head of the town. They don't do a thing about it. That is what I want you to know.
Affectionly
June Oberg

P.S. 616 4th Ave Two Harbors Minn
June Oberg

Governor Olson and his staff responded to many letters, but an answer to June is not on file.

Jan. 15, 1938

Dear GrandMa,

I hope we can see You soon. I am saving money. I have 12 cents. Did You like the Junk I sent You. I want to see your Flowers. Is it cold there. I am missing You a lot. I still love my doll. We may get a little dog. We cooked something on our little stove to-day and ate it. This is a beautiful Sunday. We took some pictures of the family. I have had a good time playing. Daddy will be home Wednesday. It is a beautiful Monday. I got some new shoes to-day and so did Phoebe. With lots of love,
Nancy Jane Perry

*   *   *

Our neighbors had a child named Brett who at age 5 developed an urge to leave home "to see the world." Brett came knocking on our back door one fine summer day carrying a brown shoebox in which he had packed one pair of undershorts, a Ken doll and a fleet of miniature cars. He told me of his plan and then asked if he could stay with us for a few days. Before I could answer, the phone rang. I answered to an hysterical mom who asked if I had seen her wandering son. I replied that he was visiting and reassured her I would send him back home. As Brett listened to my conversation, he uttered an adult-sized sigh and said, "Well, maybe next time."

Charlotte Blizen, 1950s

5-16-07

Dear Aunt Dodo,

I got such a fine baby brother yesterday morning. He weighs 8 lbs. & is quite dark. Mommie & he are doing fine, & send lots of love, as also do I. & to Uncle Harry also.

Jack Dunn

Hello!

I'm Margaret Ann the new arrival at the home of the Killy family Date August 23, 1951 Weight Six pounds

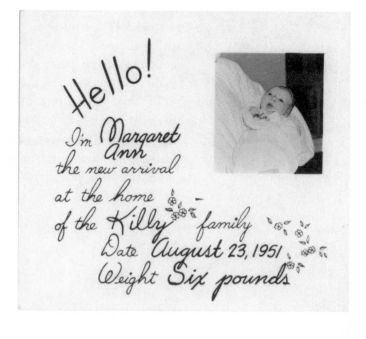

Home Life

FACING PAGE
Jack Dunn's baby brother was born May 15, 1907, and his parents made Jack's flower-garden photo into a postcard to give the big news to Aunt Dodo.

Margaret Killy starred on her own birth announcement in 1951.

Home is the core of childhood memories. What did the house look like? Was the family bursting with love? Was Rover the best dog ever, and, by the way, just what was that critter in the woodshed?

Birth

When Mother was going to have another baby, she sent me to live with her oldest sister, and her husband. They had no children and just adored me.

After my sister Emma was born on Feb. 17, 1897, my father came to get me. My uncle said, "Here comes your father." I told him to hide me so my father couldn't find me. My father said, "You better come home, Lena, you have a little sister." And I said, "I don't believe it. How could you buy me a little sister when we don't have enough money to buy bread?" He convinced me that I had a little sister and I was glad to get home. How I loved her!

Lena L. Borchardt

Abby Bartlett Weed. She arrived at 12:40 A.M. Sept. 23rd, 1902, nearly a week before she was expected. Everything was normal, and the doctor (Wm. Davis) pronounced her a perfect child. After being spanked, she gave evidence of having a fairly good pair of lungs. In looks, she is said to favor her father. Her hair was very abundant and dark brown.

*   *   *

Of course my mother, a well-educated woman and a graduate of Vassar College, believed that medicine was a science and that she must follow the rules of her pediatrician, T. L. Birnberg, especially as he had studied not only in Minnesota but in Vienna as well. Everyone knew German medical science was the best, and these were the rules: Even if the baby cries, you only feed her every four hours. No more. She is supposed to take four ounces and you weigh her before and after breast feeding to check on this. As she grows older, you add cereal and other solids and drop the 2 A.M. feeding. The child should double her birth weight in six months and triple it in one year. After she is on solid food, which in the 1920s meant that Mother personally strained all the vegetables, fruits and meats—certain foods were

Bawling baby Fredrick King was attended by his mama, Marie Madison King, in elegantly coiffed hair, and his grandma in Fulda in 1905. Dad took the photo. Do you suppose he changed diapers, too?

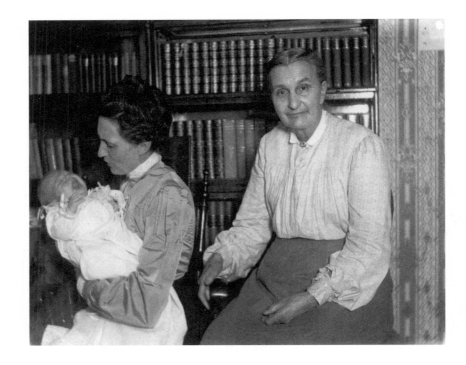

Look, but don't touch! Proud papa viewed his newborn behind glass at Minneapolis's Abbott Hospital in about 1950. Already in the 1920s, babies were increasingly born in hospitals.

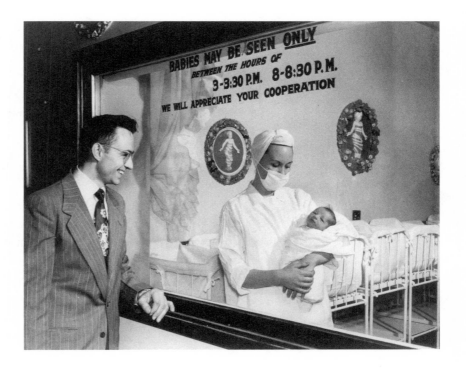

required for proper nutrition. If she doesn't eat them, you keep her in the high chair until she does, even for hours.

What if the baby is small and doesn't want four ounces? And what if she cries after three hours? You keep trying to feed her on the fourth hour, and by them she's so exhausted she falls asleep after two ounces. Picking up a crying child was also frowned on. If the child is not wet and no diaper pin is sticking in her, and the four hours haven't passed, then picking her up is forbidden. Verboten.

[My mother] Irma followed the rules and I, Ruth Harrie, didn't. I cried; I spit out solid food. I didn't gain weight as quickly as I was supposed to. I cried so much at night that Mother relented and nursed me. The doctor was angry and labeled me a feeding problem.

Ruth F. Brin, 1921

On March 7, 1943, I came screaming into the world at Maternity Hospital, not far from where most of Minneapolis' Jewish community lived. At the time, Maternity was one of only two hospitals in the Twin Cities where Jewish patients were admitted or Jewish doctors were allowed to practice medicine. (The Jewish community dealt with this problem about a decade later, by building a Jewish hospital, called Mt. Sinai, with money raised from local Jewish families.)

That March brought horrid weather, and I was born in the middle of a raging snowstorm which closed many roads. The only way my dad could come see his newborn daughter was to walk three or four miles each way through a blinding snowstorm and freezing temperatures. But he did it.

Sandra Kreamer

Parenting

[Dakota] parents did not commonly treat either their sons or their daughters harshly, and both boys and girls were taught to cultivate a self-reliant, independent spirit . . .

There was no efficient family government among the Dakotas, and severe measures were seldom resorted to for the maintenance of parental authority. The parents gave advice to their children, but fathers did not often lay their commands upon them. When they wished their children to perform any service, they usually spoke kindly to them, saying, "My son, or my daughter, will you do this?" Generally in their intercourse with their children there was a mildness of manner such as we would hardly expect to find among savages.

Some parents had great influence over their children, and others very little. Some possessed and others lacked those personal qualities which command respect and obedience. They always commended an obedient

An Ojibwe baby was held safe in a cradleboard with beautifully beaded bands. This photograph of an Ojibwe woman and child in about 1885 is part of a photo series on Native domestic life. It probably was sold to tourists.

disposition, and were pleased to have their children docile and good-natured, but they did not approve of subduing the spirit of a child by force and compelling him to submit to authority.

Samuel W. Pond, 1834

Pond was a missionary to the Dakota on the shore of Lake Calhoun, now part of Minneapolis. He and his brother, Gideon, spent nearly twenty years learning the Dakota languages and observing how they lived.

*   *   *

During the Civil War, John Henry Mitchell served with the Eleventh Regiment of Minnesota Volunteers in Tennessee, and his wife, Emma, and four young children were on their farm in Maple Grove Township, Hennepin County. John, age forty, missed them dearly. He wrote that he kept the children's pictures in his pocket "and take pleasure in looking at them every day, several times."

Dec. 28th 1864

My Dearly Beloved Wife,

. . . Emma, you spoke of the happy years we had spent together. I also look back upon the past years of our Married Life with a great deal of pleasure and satisfaction and I hope and believe that there are years of happiness yet in store for us, perhaps happier than any that have past. I think perhaps that I have told you in a letter before that I beleaved that man & wife did not know so well how to appreciate the society of each other untill they had been deprived of it. My family is my all. What cared I for all else in this world when compared with them, nothing, surely nothing.

. . . Emma, I must stop [writing]. Get allong the best you can. Kiss all the Children for me. Write soon.

Ever yours. J. H. Mitchell

John made it home from the war. He and Emma remained on the farm all their lives, with the land tended for another generation by their son Fredrick.

Lillian Brown and son Lauren clearly were nuts about each other on photo day in about 1906. See the sewing machine to the right? Lillian may have been hard at work for the family or for income. She went on to be a matron on the Albert Lea police force.

My father was away a good deal in August 1867, and once as he drove home he said, "Walter! You are to have a new mother. Whom do you think it is? It is Miss Hattie Harwood."

Shortly before [step]mother Fannie died, she, with true wifely concern for father's interests, approved a wife to take her place, providing the lady would be willing. Mother Fannie knew that father couldn't get on alone. He, with indifferent health, couldn't have the whole care of [step]sister Matie and me. The choice fell upon Miss Harwood, and so in later summer father proposed marriage and was accepted.

The news . . . set me wild with joy. I knew Miss Harwood as almost an angel. I thot of the happy Sunday School hours I had spent the year before under her teaching. She was handsome beyond common, a great point with me; besides she was goodness itself.

Imagination ran riot as to the good times coming, and they didn't come short of expectation. Father was easier about work requirements. I spent days playing with my prospective cousin, Willis Thompson, at his grandfather's home about 1225 5th St. S.E., Minneapolis . . .

Miss Harwood always had talked of genuine love to us boys in Sunday School, and now she was to come to us, was to love me as her own child. I was to have the wonderful thing I had missed for ten years—Whole-hearted love, tho it was to be tempered with good judgment . . .

It was a happy evening in October when father brot home Mother Hattie. The dining table took on a homelike look, for mother was a good housekeeper.

Unbelievable delight for me! Here was the angel of my dreams, the one who had taught me to know the meaning of simple love as between friends. She was my mother. I was to have her for always. All my griefs were over. At table I sat beside her, got hold of her hand, and in short behaved like a small child, tho 15. From now on, sunshine and cheer were in our home. I was watched for overstrain, and tho I worked hard much as usual, mother saw that I was not overworked. There were play spells. Sore fingers were done up. Warm mittens were made and mended, and besides that, the cooking was good, the food in plenty and suitable. Mother graced the home.

Walter Stone Pardee, 1867

Another loving family: Mrs. Jay W. Hanlon and her children, Edward and Sheila, of St. Paul in about 1930. A society woman, she has her hair marcelled—that is, set in a distinctive deep wave.

A mother and son in about 1905. Imagine caring for a child in her long, white dress and Gibson girl hairdo. No spit-up on that shoulder! His romper also was immaculate.

Babies, babies, babies, at the Children's Home Society of Minnesota in St. Paul in about 1940. All were available for adoption.

"What did you used to do mamma, before you were married?" asked a little four year old. "Well, my dear, I had a very good time." "A good time!" he exclaimed indignantly, *"what, without me!"*

The Minnesota Pupil, February 3, 1869

Evidence is mounting that the Minnesota Valley is the most prolific of the State. Triplets were recently born to Mrs. Henry Mangles, of LeSueur, to another lady in Tyron, and a third to the lower part of Nicollet.

St. Paul Pioneer, August 6, 1874

This world produces no other beauty; no other object of interest; no other more lovely nor lovable thing, than a bright, sweet, confiding little child. What heart has not strangely thrilled when a little one came to his knee at the day's close, placed its dimpled little hand in his, and looked up with that sweet, earnest, enquiring gaze, so nearly that of an angel, from another and better sphere? . . . When we place our arm around the precious little form and nestle it close to our breast, how a silent prayer, unmarred by feeble words, goes up in its behalf.

Uncle Dudley's Odd Hours, by M. C. Russell of Duluth, 1882

LITTLE IMMIGRANTS. Last Tuesday two little girls age 11 and 12 arrived here in Minneapolis from the southern part of Sweden. They had traveled all that long way alone and were on their way to join their parents in North Dakota. The girls' names are Hilda and Freda Sorenson. A tag, bearing their names and the address to which they were destined, was fastened around the neck of each. They had crossed the ocean aboard the Thingvalla liner

In 1905, a Windom
commercial photographer,
Benjamin P. Skewis, found
an entertaining way to
pose a man and a well-
balanced child.

B. P. Skewis   WINDOM MINN.

One of Duluthians Franklin
and Dorothy King's three
children—Sheila, Phillip,
or Ralph—had both a
scooter and a playpen
in the mid-1950s. Young
children of both genders
wore the little white shoes
in that era. This one has
a Kewpie doll curl. Dad
was an industrial engineer;
mom worked at a local
bank. The woman to the
left wore the ubiquitous
apron and open-toed
shoes.

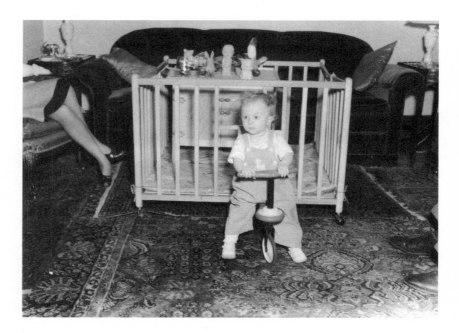

"Island" [Iceland] and their agents have taken care of the little "misses" wherever they have passed, making sure that they boarded the right trains.

Translated from Svenska Amerikanska Posten, a
Swedish-language newspaper, September 13, 1892

A diminutive immigrant by the name of John Amundson, 12 years of age, arrived here [Minneapolis] from Trondhjon, Norway. He carried a card around his neck addressed to Amund Richardson, Minneapolis, Minn., but no such person has been found yet. The boy says that his father, who sent his ticket, and his two sisters, Maria and Johanna, are in this country. He is in the care of the city officials for the time being.

Translated from Svenska Amerikanska Posten, December 27, 1892

My home life [in Albert Lea] was, I suspect, somewhat normal for the times and considering the low economic status of the family. Dad was never close to us children. He never talked to us as a father or played with us. He was always distant & considered us somewhat as competition for food at the table and attention from friends & relatives. I don't ever recall receiving from dad any advice about life or grades in school or anything of significance. He never talked with us about anything. Mother never did either, for that matter. We grew up learning from our friends and in school. I was never

A farm father and his son wore their overalls for a studio portrait, probably in about 1910. Usually people in that time dressed up for photos, but perhaps this man wanted to show justifiable pride in his work. Notice his protective hand on the boy's shoulder. Or is he reining him in?

advised to do good in school by my parents. Regardless of the grades I would bring home on my report cards, mother would never even notice, it seemed, the low grades, but signed the cards & gave the report card back. I recall that she had to come to school one time when I was having trouble with arithmetic in second grade. The teacher wanted to show her about my problem, but nothing ever resulted from her visit.

Robert D. Hill, 1930s

Sun. September 30, 1934. J. P. Smith, attorney from Mankato, came this evening to see mother. He is going to try to get mother a divorce tomorrow.

Mon. October 1. Started to school today. Went downtown to the Court House. I was a witness at daddy & mother's divorce trial. The divorce was granted. I was sorry to have them divorced. It was very cold and snowy today. I have a very bad cold.

William M. Cummings

It seemed to me that [Daddy and I] talked about everything, but now that I think back, I know we really only talked about my life. I could tell Daddy all the things that I kept secret from Mama. Like about the time Donald Callender and I lay down on one of the pews in the back of the church whispering quietly so his sister, Danetta, couldn't find us. Of course, she started crying, and pretty soon we heard Reverend Callender calling Donald. Well, that was the end of that, but I sure was mad at Danetta and I told Daddy so. He thought it was funny. He must have thought a lot of

William Gardner, his wife Rosella, and their daughter, also named Rosella, may have been spending a Sunday visiting family when this picture was shot in St. Paul in 1939. He looked sharp in his double-breasted suit.

28

things were funny, 'cause he laughed a lot. Except when he said, "Ba,'"—I was nicknamed for Mama's sister Alice, who was known as Babe—"Ba,' your Daddy sure loves you." I'd always frown and say, "I *know* that, Daddy." I acted as if it made me angry, but a warmth filled me every time he said it. And it still does, just thinking about it.

Evelyn Fairbanks, about 1934

A happy dad bounced his baby on his knee in about 1945. The wallpaper was a floral repeat, so popular mid-century.

Gerald Wayne Chicog in a charming cradleboard with beadwork bands was admired by his grandparents on the Nett Lake Reservation in September 1946.

Mother watched the children play in about 1900. Who of us would allow kids in ruffled clothes to frolic on the lawn today? Oh, and is the big guy on the right a bit miffed? Maybe he wasn't allowed to join in.

Siblings

One time I recall that we four younger children were playing "Keep House" in a big packing box upstairs. (We moved so often that packing boxes were always carefully saved for the next moving.) [Her father was a minister.] Someone's toes got stepped on. Ida, the baby cousin, began to cry. Her sister Ella thought I had stepped on her, which made her mad and she hit me. I naturally hit back and all four of us began to cry. Then Cousin Hattie used her elder sister privilege of punishing me in defence of her sister, and my brother June was equally ready to assert his family rights as my protector. There followed such a hullabaloo, such an uncivil engagement of fists, and above all, such howling, that I wonder why the neighbors didn't come rushing into the parsonage.

Our two mothers rushed upstairs to quiet the melee. In the hasty trial that followed, no one was able to decide who was to blame; but it was the consensus of opinion that Hattie and I were the chief offenders. So we two were ordered by Aunt Cord to stand, each of us in a corner, until we should be willing to say we were sorry. I suppose I would have been standing there yet if Hattie hadn't taken the first step. We walked slowly to the middle of the room and kissed each other as ordered and said we were sorry. My conscience troubled me only because I had told a lie. I think Hattie was sorry, for she was the kind of a child who was always held up as an example for all other children, and she deserved it.

Anna Lathrop Clary, late 1860s

Brothers Gerhard and Irwin Ellestad of Lanesboro, all duded up in about 1903. Those hats were called straw boaters, the kind worn at carnivals and fairs.

She liked him, but did he like her? This was back in about 1935. They both could have used a bath after a lovely day at the lake or playground.

I will tell of a melon episode with [step]sister Matie that summer [when he was fifteen]. She was 6 and as an only child was rather spoiled. She and I differed so much that [step]mother couldn't keep peace between us, and seeing she always took Matie's part, I felt abused. So Matie was fair game if a chance came to bother her, especially as always she ran to mother to tell. I was disgusted and felt that sometimes at least my side should have won but it never did, and so I took the only means at hand to get even and this meant misleading Matie to my advantage. One of my grievances was that I never could have a thing but she demanded the best of it, and I wouldn't give it to her so she ran to mother about it.

To offset this, one day I brot in a watermelon—a poor one with a big [end] and a little end. There was little fit to eat in any part of the melon and none at all in the small end. Our melon patch that summer was a failure, but I had found this little runt and meant to eat what there was good in it.

Matie came along, and she must have some. There was none to spare, not enough for one person, much less two. I said, "You can't have any." "I'll tell mother." "O well, I suppose you must have some but you can't have any of the nice little end." "Yes, I want the little end." And she got it. It was mean of me for in the little end was hardly a tinge of red. Of course I had the big end, which was rather good, and of course after the melon was gone I told her the facts.

Walter Stone Pardee, 1866

Nothing like a little brotherly hair brushing. Ouch! He could have paid more attention to his britches than to her hair.

Names

In the 1800s, when a child named for an ancestor died young, it was customary—almost obligatory—to give the same name to the next-born child of the same gender. That's why "Alexander" or "Sarah," for example, may keep popping up in your family genealogy.

The custom of naming a child after a deceased husband or wife from a previous marriage was used very early (by about AD 1000) among the Vikings of Scandinavia and continued in early Minnesota.

*   *   *

EDWARD NEILL, WHO SERVED PRESIDENT ABRAHAM LINCOLN, NAMED HIS DAUGHTER MINNESOTA NEILL.

*   *   *

Minnesota settlers bestowed creative names upon its places—cities, counties, creeks, townships, and so on. For example, Flora, a township in Renville County, was named for the first horse in town. Darfur, a city in Watonwan County, was named either for a region of Sudan or in honor of a question from one Scandinavian railroad man to another: "Why you stop dar fur?" No kidding. That's according to Minnesota Place Names *by Warren Upham, a fascinating read.*

Most place names were in honor of early settlers, distinguished men, or geographic features. Indians named some places in their languages, of course, and the names stuck. Children inspired some names. Whether the honored children were young or grown isn't always known. Some places still exist; others don't.

You might wonder why Virginia, a city in St. Louis County, isn't included. That's because it was named not for a female but for the region's virgin forest.

Ada. City, Norman County. Named in 1881 in honor of a daughter of William H. Fisher of St. Paul, a lawyer and superintendent of the St. Paul and Pacific Railroad. He was in charge of the rail line in the Red River Valley. Ada Nelson Fisher died in 1880 at the age of six of diarrhea, a common killer at the time.

Boy Lake. Township, Cass County. Translated from the Ojibwe name for the boys killed by the Dakota during a conflict between the two tribes in about 1768. Three little boys were killed while gathering wild rice.

Burnsville. City, Dakota County. Named for its first settlers, William Burns and his wife and five sons, who emigrated from Canada in 1853. The family originally spelled the name *Byrnes*, and the place name on some old records is Byrnesville.

Esther. Township, Polk County. For the daughter of President Grover Cleveland.

Luverne. City, Rock County. To honor Eva Luverne Hawes, born in 1857, eldest daughter of the first settler, Philo Hawes. Her father's cousin, Lucy Cotter of Red Wing, supposedly read the name in a novel or romance magazine and requested that the baby be so named.

Medford. Township, Steele County. The first township meeting was held at the house of William K. Colling, an Englishman who had arrived in 1854 and had taken a homestead claim. He said that he had a son born on board the ship *Medford.* The boy was named in honor of the ship, and Colling proposed that the town should be named in honor of the boy.

Otto. Post office, Pope County, 1867–89. Named for the youngest son of the first settler and postmaster, Norman Shook.

Verndale. City, Wadena County. Named in honor of Helen Vernette "Vernie" Smith, a granddaughter of Lucas W. Smith, first postmaster, in 1878.

I was so unfortunate as to be the youngest of five children who, soon after I was born, was left motherless. I had to bear the humiliating name "Hakadah," meaning "the pitiful last," until I should earn a more dignified and appropriate name. I was regarded as little more than a plaything by the rest of the children.

But after four years, the boy was renamed.

In memory of this victory, the boy would now receive his name. A loud "Ho-o-o" of approbation reverberated from the edge of the forest upon the Minnesota's bank.

Half frightened, the little fellow was now brought into the circle, looking very much as if he were about to be executed. Cheer after cheer went up for the awe-stricken boy. Chankpee-yuhah, the medicine man, proceeded to confer the name.

"Ohiyesa (or Winner) shall be thy name henceforth. Be brave, be patient, and thou shall always win! Thy name is Ohiyesa."

Charles Eastman, 1858

The [native] mother names the infant very much as we name a town. She usually gives birth to the child in the bushes, and if beneath a pine tree would call it "Pine Tree," but if a bird happened to be in it at the time she would call it "Sitting Bird" or "Flying Bird" or "Singing Bird," as the case might be. These names are temporary. If the child should be sick, someone is chosen to select a name for it, and if the child gets well it always retains the name, although it may take other names, either selected by itself or by other persons . . .

Self-naming is the most marked and unique event in an Indian's life, and is as follows: After the child arrives at puberty, if the boy, the father, if a girl, the mother, instead of placing before the child its portion of food as usual substitutes charcoal. The child knows what this is for; he must fast. So he goes into the woods and hides himself, where he stays until he falls asleep and dreams of some animal, and that animal not only gives him a name, but he is supposed to be under the good influences of that animal for life. Sometimes these fasts continue for days and sometimes they are short . . . If a child dreams of the red fox, it is supposed he will become possessed of all the alertness, slyness and trickery of that animal . . .

Department of the Interior Census Office, 1890

November 1932
Mr. Floyd B. Olson

Dear Governor,

Just a line to say we always listen to the Farm Labor talks over the Radio and we want you to know that we are 100 per. for you, and we sure hope you will be re-elected.

We have named our baby boy after you and hope he will grow up to be as a courageous young man as you are.

Respectfully yours

Mr. and Mrs. Bernhard Olson

4139 Toledo Ave.

Robbinsdale, Minn.

A two-year-old orator in St. Paul caught the eye of a newspaper photographer in about 1937. The tot was named Floyd B. Olson, undoubtedly for the then recent Minnesota governor.

The most popular given names in the United States, from 1880 to 1960

Boys

1880: John, William, Charles, George, James, Joseph, Frank, Henry, Thomas, Harry.

1890: John, William, James, George, Charles, Joseph, Frank, Harry, Henry, Edward.

1900: John, William, James, George, Charles, Joseph, Frank, Henry, Robert, Harry.

1910: John, William, James, Robert, Joseph, Charles/George (tie), Edward, Frank, Henry.

1920: John, William, James, Robert, Joseph, Charles, George, Edward, Thomas, Frank.

1930: Robert, James, John, William, Richard, Charles, Donald, George, Joseph, Edward.

1940: James, Robert, John, William, Richard, Charles, David, Thomas, Donald, Ronald.

1950: John, James, Robert, William, Michael, David, Richard, Thomas, Charles, Gary.

1960: David, Michael, John, James, Robert, Mark, William, Richard, Thomas, Steven.

Girls

1880: Mary, Anna, Elizabeth, Margaret, Minnie, Emma, Martha, Alice, Marie, Annie/Sarah (tie).

1890: Mary, Anna, Elizabeth, Emma, Margaret, Rose, Ethel, Florence, Ida, Bertha/Helen (tie).

1900: Mary, Helen, Anna, Margaret, Ruth, Elizabeth, Marie, Rose, Florence, Bertha.

1910: Mary, Helen, Margaret, Dorothy, Ruth, Anna, Mildred, Elizabeth, Alice, Ethel.

1920: Mary, Dorothy, Helen, Margaret, Ruth, Virginia, Elizabeth, Anna, Mildred, Betty.

1930: Mary, Betty, Dorothy, Helen, Barbara, Margaret, Maria, Patricia, Doris, Joan/Ruth (tie).

1940: Mary, Barbara, Patricia, Carol, Judith, Betty, Nancy, Maria, Margaret, Linda.

1950: Linda, Mary, Patricia, Barbara, Susan, Maria, Sandra, Nancy, Deborah, Kathleen.

1960: Mary, Susan, Maria, Karen, Lisa, Linda, Donna, Patricia, Debra, Deborah.

Coming to Minnesota

Between 1849 and 1858, Minnesota was the fastest growing place in the United States. Don't imagine there were flocks of babies. No, it was people pushing into the new Minnesota Territory.

Until 1850, most people living in Minnesota were Indians—primarily Dakota and Ojibwe. English was only the fourth most commonly spoken language. Ahead of English were French, thanks to the fur trade, and two Indian languages, Dakota and Ojibwe. By the time Minnesota became a state in 1858, English was tops.

*   *   *

In the spring of 1900, fifteen-year-old Maude Baumann and her family packed up a covered wagon and moved way north in Minnesota. Her father said they were in quest of some land to call their own. They left Waltham, in southern Minnesota's Mower County, to settle near Bagley in Clearwater County. The trip took three weeks and two days. Today it would take about six hours by car. Maude kept a journal to send to relatives in Mower County.

Apr. 22. We are in Dundas, Minn., a town about 11 miles northeast of Faribault. I said last night Father was looking for another camping place, but he happened to talk to the clerk of the Modern Woodsman Lodge, and he told him to go ahead and build our fire. We did, and thanks to his kindness nobody molested [bothered] us. We thot Faribault was noisy, not being used to big towns, and every hour of the night the big clock in the court-house steeple disturbed us. People take us for horse-traders.

Moving day (or month)! A family stood by a covered wagon in about 1880. They probably were getting ready to hit the road, saying good-bye to family and friends. A classic pose of the times was to stand in front of house or wagon, showing the family's possessions.

April 23. This finds us in Farmington. Have traveled 28 miles today. Passed thru Northfield. There are three bridges over the river. We drove out on the middle one. Thot the scenery was very nice. Today we went about a mile out of our way on account of a marsh. Father thot it contained some 400 acres. Last night we were invited to a Mr. Kreger's to hear some music. Two guitars and a mandolin. We enjoyed that, and they asked us to write to them and tell them whether we arrived safely at our new home. We're not so lucky tonight. There aren't so many trees here. It's not so pretty as some of the places we've passed by. Went by Cannon Falls, Castle Rock and Northfield before we reached this place. The people where we are camped saved us building a fire. They told us to boil our coffee there, and Mother and the Baby are inside. Baby keeps good, but gets very tired riding, and is so pleased to get ou[t] of the wagon and run around.

People are very kind. If we always find such nice folks we'll be all right.

Morning. Father keeps our dog tied under the wagon nights, and he barks if anyone comes near the wagon. It is lovely this morning. Will reach the cities [St. Paul and Minneapolis] if all goes well.

Apr. 25. Two days since I wrote. We are about 8 miles north of Minneapolis. We thought we would never find our way out of that city. We camped the latest [hour] last night we have yet. Father could not find a livery stable and if some men had not let him put the horse in their barn, I don't know what we would have done. Jim [the horse] was so afraid of the street-cars that we dared not stay on Cedar Bridge Ave. as we were directed to do.

We saw steamboats on the Mississippi, which doesn't seem to very wide here. But logs! That river is just full of floating logs. Some have crowded together and stopped the others, and men are working to loosen them. As we drive along the river, we can see hundreds and hundreds of logs. We are driving up the west side of the river.

Minneapolis is a very nice place, but we were called "hayseeds" there, which is suited us not at all. Anyway the many sights we saw repaid us for coming this way. We stayed in one of the quietest parts of the city last night, so had a good night's rest. We always sleep in our wagon with our dog on guard. We would have lost a wagon tire in the city, if a kindly disposed dray-man had not stopped us in time to save a lot of bother. We have camped for dinner. The Lady of the house brought us out some boiled potatoes. Glory be, we needn't cook any. We always camp near homes on account of drinking water, and we have to buy milk for the Baby.

Wish we had a camera. We can still watch the logs on the river. The river looked wider here.

Three years later, Maude was the first teacher in a new school in district seventy-five, seven and a half miles southeast of Bagley. She reported that there was no school in January and February because of the severe winters.

Aleck is 1 year old. Yossel is 2 and [Uncle] Fishel is 18. [Father] Shimon has tickets and papers galore. [Mother] Maryam is hanging on to two children and [Grandmother] Baube Rochal and Fishel are gathering bundles. Shimon has been told that his piano box full of household furnishings did not arrive with the train to Minneapolis. The train left New York with everything aboard, but 24 hours later when the train arrived in Chicago where the transfer was made to Minneapolis, the piano box simply did not make the transfer. Time will tell if it arrives.

In Minneapolis, the Jewish community had a committee for meeting newcomers. The committee consisted of I. S. Joseph, Joe Schanfield and a few others who took turns meeting trains each afternoon at the Milwaukee Depot on Washington Avenue, the hub of Jewish employment. So it was that Joe Schanfield and I. S. Joseph walked a block or two to meet the trains.

I was never told how it was known when comers were arriving; however, the family was met and taken to an apartment on Fifth Street, just off of

Displaced children at the Jewish Sheltering Home, Minneapolis, in about 1925. Check out the bowl haircuts. Isn't it amazing how the same hairstyle can make people look similar?

Eleventh Avenue South. This was the hub of the south-side ghetto and an easy walk to Washington Avenue. A horse and wagon hauled them the short distance.

This apartment building had only four flats. It had five rooms and a kitchen all by itself! It had a "bathroom" which had a toilet whose water box was up near the ceiling with a pull chain to get the water to flush. It had a space for the galvanized tub the family brought for bathing. Never had the Schwartz family seen such amenities and can you imagine what else? The smell? Well, they were told it was called fresh air.

Fannie S. Schanfield, 1908

My boyhood home in South Minneapolis was in a comfortable middle-class neighborhood. Father, upon retirement from our Asbury, Iowa, dairy farm in 1909, had purchased a four-bedroom house at 3105 [South] Clinton Avenue in Minneapolis. His main objective was to enroll my older sister, Leone, at the University of Minnesota and to enable my brother, Harold, and me to attend Minneapolis Public Schools.

Railroads were very cooperative in assisting farm families to move cross-country at the turn of the century. They would provide a boxcar to ship uncrated household goods. If 25 percent of the shipment included farm machinery and animals and was accompanied by a caretaker, the tariff was very low. So my father loaded our furniture along with a buggy, sleigh and Fanny, Leone's riding horse, in a freight car in Dubuque, Iowa, and made the three-day boxcar trip to Minneapolis . . .

Only two blocks away, at Fourth Avenue and Lake Street, there was a convenient shopping center: two grocery stores, a meat market, drug store, café, barber shop, tailor shop, candy store, doctor, dentist, florist, electrician, printer, bicycle shop, bakery and shoe maker. All the businesses seemed to be owner-operated and willing employers of some kids.

Carl Warmington

A girl took a photograph of a family near Lake of the Woods in about 1912. The simple, inexpensive Kodak Brownie camera became widely popular about then, introducing the concept of a snapshot. This family's home was easily transported to provide shelter during times of fishing, berry picking, maple sugaring, and hunting.

Homes

My parents came from the New England states, in or about the year 1855, and settled upon a homestead near Rochester, where, on September 8, 1857, I was born.

The cabin in which I first saw daylight was constructed of logs and contained one room. The furnishings were principally home made. The sideboard was true to its name, in as much as it was a board fastened to the side of the cabin, upon two wooden pins that were driven into the logs, at a convenient height from the floor.

Walter F. Benjamin

The [St. Paul] house [called Trout Brook, for the fish-rich water running through the property] was situated on a hill in the center of a 45-acre

Luckily, these girls had each other and their china-head dolls for company. It must have been lonesome out there in eastern Clay County in about 1910.

tract completely surrounded by a picket fence. It might be interesting to you to know how the property was acquired. My father had long wanted to buy it from the owner, Mr. Phalen, who refused to sell. One day very unexpectedly, he appeared at my father's office and wished to sell, asking $400, the money to be given him at once. Father, not being prepared at that time to buy, borrowed the money and bought the land. Later he learned the reason for this change of mind, which was due to the fact that Mr. Phalen had committed a murder and was obliged to leave town that day.

This land was bounded on the west by Mississippi Street, on the north by York Street, on the east by the Arlington Hill district and on the south were the railroad tracks. By damming the brook, Father made an artificial lake covering nearly an acre, on the shore of which was a boat house large enough to hold three boats, also a bathing house where we learned to swim. In the winter, we enjoyed the skating. Many happy times of my girlhood were spent when a club of young men, friends of my five brothers, would come out from the City several times each winter, bringing their young lady friends and a band of musicians, to spend the evening skating. Bonfires would be built around the lake, and it was all very beautiful. Even though younger than most of the group, I never lacked partners, as with such an opportunity to practice, I excelled on the ice.

There was much natural beauty to the land, and Father had a German gardener who added to this beauty by his landscaping and making many gravel walks and rustic bridges. A plum orchard near the brook was a perfect fairyland in the spring when in blossom. A summer house, with latticed sides and benches all around, was built on a hill, and there was always a cool breeze to be enjoyed there.

Maria Rice Dawson, 1870s

When I was five, in 1881, Mother had built a home in south Minneapolis, about 45 minutes out by horse-car. There was no bath[room], no city water, no sewer. The house had twelve rooms and a big shed which was part of the main house and finished on the outside the same as the house . . .

On the back of the kitchen stove, with its four griddles and an oven, was a reservoir holding about four or five gallons of water. That was kept filled with rainwater and used for dishwashing. The reservoir, like the stove, was black iron, with a top in two sections; when closed, it made a good place to keep things warm.

Mother and daughter posed in the luxurious parlor of the James Blaisdell home, at Twenty-fourth Street and Nicollet Avenue, in about 1890. Signs of wealth are everywhere: The portrait rests on a gold easel. The woman wears an elegant dress. The stuffed bird reflects the upper crust's interest in natural history.

A girl sat reading and two women conversed in the parlor of the Josiah B. Chaney residence, 604 Rondo Avenue, St. Paul, in about 1899. It might well be that the visiting child was instructed to sit still and be quiet.

On the kitchen table there sat a large pail of well water, with a dipper in it, and all winter one had to break the ice to get the dipper out in the mornings, as there was no heat in the kitchen once the supper dishes were finished and the stove banked for the night. The big hard-coal stove in the dining room, with its lovely, cheery isinglass windows, glowed steadily for six or seven months each year, and in winter the dining room was where we lived. We did our lessons there, brother Cholly and I, and Mother sewed and read there, while Ed—our stepfather—went over his guns and decoy ducks, fishing tackle and all the equipment of his active outdoor life. The dining table in winter became a library table where we gathered to pursue our various tasks and interests by the light of two huge oil lamps, one at either end.

Our parlor was never opened in winter, for there was no stove, nor any room for one.

Blanche Stoddard Seely

Mother was a genius at homemaking wherever she went. She always had wonderful food, even when we had the greenest, most mediocre cook. Being a born cook herself and loving it, Mother could always train girls in a short time. There were always comfortable places to sit and good reading lights and books and magazines galore. She was what one would call an easy-going housekeeper. She disliked intensely what she called "dirt chasers" and always claimed that you never found a comfortable home or good food where the homemaker was always chasing dirt and peering in corners. I think there is lots to be said for this theory.

All I know is that no two children could have been brought up in a more comfortable, pleasant, delightful home atmosphere than Anson and I were. I expect the fact that Mother had had such an unhappy childhood made her want to do everything for us. Our house was always the center of everything. All the children of the neighborhood congregated there because Mother would let us do about anything, in the way of mussing up the house. She would much rather have us there where she knew what we were doing than off some place where she didn't. I can remember that one whole winter when we had the stamp craze, we kept a stamp store in Mother's bedroom with troops of children trailing in. Another winter when we were having a dry spell financially (as we often did) [her father was an attorney], we rented [out] 1623 Third Avenue and boarded at the Judd House. Mother had in her bedroom all that winter my large dolls' house at one end, and at the other Anson's carpenter bench on a sheet.

Margaret Jackson Bovey, 1890s

Going to the new homestead with father

So it was that we looked forward to, on June 2, 1902. We had lived in Bemidji, and now we were going to make a homestead. Boyhood chums at Bemidji had all wished us well. The tamarack swamp where we played was hard to part with.

Father and I boarded the slow train in the early morning. [His mother and sister would move later.] The rails for this had just recently been laid. Cave-ins were frequent, and the 20 miles to Blackduck passed slowly. The caboose was crowded with mostly homesteaders. I was the only boy aboard and got kidded about my little pack sack made out of flour sacks.

We had some lunch and soon started out on our 12-mile hike. I had never walked 12 miles in my life, but was game to try. Father and I walked 5 miles straight north on what was called the "Range Line" road . . . We waded in mud all the way, as this was the wettest year ever. Walked logs over water-holes and about 5 P.M. we reached the South Cormorant River at the Peterson place. Here there was a new trail running mostly east past the Miller Brothers' place.

When we got to Joe Miller's, it had clouded up real black. Joe took a fresh chaw of tobacco and invited us in for the night. Homesteaders were always hospitable, and we were tempted to stay, but Auntie Rebecca [who had moved there earlier to help his father] had been waiting for us alone for some days, so we push[ed] on.

The trail soon petered out and was just a succession of blaze marks on trees. Then the storm broke and soon we were soaked. Father would work ahead, looking for the next blaze on a tree while I stayed at the blaze we had found. We were in a heavy electrical storm and knew we had to watch what we were doing or we'd be lost. Brush was very thick, and that bothered us.

Be it ever so humble: this homestead stood in the woods near Blackduck Lake in about 1901. The family may have been showing off their homestead expansion.

But every step was nearer home, and finally we joined another stream that father was familiar with. And now we had to ford a stream. We just strode in. We couldn't get any wetter. Now we were on a good path and made our sodden way wearily. Then we came to the well, with the cover floating, and here was that haven of a 12×12 tarpaper shack, and plump Auntie Rebecca in the doorway, waving.

How do two grown people and a 10-year-old boy manage to live in a 12×12 shack? The door in the middle faced south, the window was west of it, about 18 inches square. Two beds filled the back of the room. The stove was in the east end. A 3-foot by 3-foot table was hinged to the wall on the west side and was held up by one leg with a spike through the table into the leg. When not used for a table, it was dropped down. Every inch was used. Boxes were nailed to the wall. All the space under the beds was used. The tiny cook stove was booming, and we were glad to shed our sopping clothes. We should have taken the wagon road from Petersons' but thought the trail was shorter. Dear old Auntie was overjoyed to see us, and we were pretty happy ourselves.

Robert C. Shaw

The neighborhood kids gathered on the first day of school in 1950, waiting for the yellow bus to take them to Brimhall Elementary. The two little ones in front were too young for school but got to be in the photo anyway. The children were gathered at the corner of Arona Avenue and Ruggles Street in Falcon Heights, then a new suburb north of St. Paul. This was the generation known as "war babies," followed by "baby boomers."

The legend is that Father sprung a surprise at the dinner table one evening. He asked, "How would you like to live on the Island?" Then he took a vote, and our response was a unanimous "aye!"

And so, for the next twenty-six years that romantic spot became our summer home. But first it must be made ready for all ten of us. Besides our little grandmother we were Fred, Betty, Phil, Dick, Kate, me (Isabel), Marg and Father and Mother. Ages 18 down the scale to 6.

The house, built in 1873 and modeled after the octagon home of the writer J. G. Holland on the Connecticut River in Springfield, Mass., had two additions by the time we took it over. Father expanded it thusly: The icehouse was moved to the lower part of the island, and a dining room, kitchen and den took up that space, with four bedrooms and bath above. But he left intact the two-story octagonal front part with its encircling porches and its fascinating outside stairway. Whatever the weather, we must go outdoors to get to bed, and how we children loved that!

. . . Marg and I looked forward all winter long, in our ordinary home in Minneapolis, to the day in June when we would come home from Douglas school to pack our bags and set off on the Minnetonka streetcar for a glorious summer on THE ISLAND.

Isabel Shephard Tryon Thibault, 1910s

Two kids, two kittens, and a bowl of milk—a fine party in 1915

Animals

The kitten I brought with me when we moved into the woods proved to be the most intelligent cat my mother ever saw. His name was Tommy. He and [the dog] Pomp, like the lion and the lamb, would lie down together and play together. While Eddie was sitting on the floor, Tommy was great company for him. He would submit to anything from the baby, let him pull his tail or ears, or poke his fingers in his eyes—do anything he liked and seemed to enjoy it. But if one of the older boys tried any rough handling, Tommy would resent it instantly.

I regret to record that after two or three years, Tommy disappeared and we never saw him again. It was a real sorrow to me as I loved him. I never set my affections on another cat, though he was replaced by another. He couldn't fill Tommy's place with any of the family, but he could catch mice, which is the real function of a cat, I suppose.

Anna Lathrop Clary, 1860s

I brought home a few bedbugs [from a classmate's house] and later we had a fight to catch them. The bedbug is a troublesome insect of an offensive smell which infests the crevices of a bedstead. About the best way to kill them is to scatter snuff around, and when you hear them sneeze, go after them with a blow-torch.

June Clary in a letter to his sister Anna, 1860s

Batiste Gahbow showed her prizewinning 4-H hog at the Mille Lacs Indian Reservation in about 1930. Later known as Batiste Sam, she was a longtime elder at Mille Lacs and a guide at the Mille Lacs Indian Museum.

We had many curious wild pets. There were young foxes, bears, wolves, raccoons, fawns, buffalo calves and birds of all kinds, tamed by various boys. My pets were different at different times, but I particularly remember one. I once had a grizzly bear for a pet and so far as he and I were concerned, our relations were charming and very close. But I hardly know whether he made more enemies for me or I for him. It was his habit to treat every boy unmercifully who injured me. He was despised for his conduct in my interest and I was hated on account of his interference.

Charles Eastman, 1860s

HOSPITAL FOR PETS—Several little misses (mere children) created no little amusement yesterday by holding a fair in a stable in Upper Town for the benefit of sick pets. They sold tickets at five cents each, and had quite a full attendance of ladies and gentlemen. The receipts from refreshment tables and tickets amounted to over $7.00 They have decided to take the money and build a two-story miniature hospital for weakly toads, sick kittens, and all other ailing pets. It is to be known as the "Charles Dickens Hospital for Sick Pets."

St. Paul Daily Press, June 14, 1868

One year in the early fall, my mother made me a new dress. She ripped up an old linsey-woolsey, washed it, turned it wrong side out, and, by adding some other old material to it, made quite a respectable garment.

I put it on one afternoon and just after dark I went out to the woodshed. My foot touched something soft [a skunk!] and I was saluted by a most terrific odor. It enveloped me, almost overpowered me. But I got into the house—only to be greeted by shouts of dismay. Everyone rushed to open doors and windows. The children held their noses. [My brother] June ran out to try to waylay and shoot the invader, but he had disappeared and was never again heard from or better—never again smelled.

I had to strip, take a bath, hair and all. My clothes were carried out and hung on the line. But in the morning when we went out to get them from the line, they were still odiferous. The white garments were washed and boiled and came out all right. But alas! My dress! Ma washed and aired it, but still it smelled. So she buried it, having heard that the earth would absorb the smell. But no! It could never be worn again. Everything in the house smelled for several days. Even our food seemed contaminated. But the crowning absurdity of all was the cookies. We had some in a covered earthenware jar. The first bite was enough, too much. So we took them out and offered them to Old Star who was very fond of cookies. But even she turned up her cow nose and walked away.

Anna Lathrop Clary, 1860s

Clark Smith's handsome two-year-old moose is dead. Last Saturday morning he got hold of a box of crackers which had been thrown away. The crackers must have been worse than Mark Twain's manuscript, which even a camel could not digest. They caked on the moose's stomach, and the favorite pet died Sunday morning. Mr. Smith had refused $250 for the animal, which was a splendid specimen of his tribe.

Grand Rapids Magnet, April 11, 1893

Almost ready to race through the streets of Tower in about 1900, the Coffey cousins and Major the Dog show off their homemade cart, with a wooden shipping box for the driver's seat. The children are, left to right, Angela Coffey, Kathleen Coffey, William Oppel, Emmett Coffey, Callista Coffey, and Douglas Coffey.

We had a real good dog named Rover. He would pull us all over on a sled. He was part bull dog. If it was icy, sometimes two of us would get on the sled. Mother would send us to Central Avenue [in Minneapolis] for groceries and we'd be home in no time and that was five blocks away. We had a couple of little stores that were real close by. One day George and I were out with the dog and sled, and about a block from our house a boy sicked [sicced] his dog after ours and the dogs started to fight and ours was still hitched to the sled. The owner of the dog was so angry. He came out with a gun and wanted to shoot our dog, so George put his arms around our dog's neck and the other dog bit George thru the hand. I ran home for Mother. I was so frightened that I was just petrified and it seems that I just couldn't run. Mother brought a pail of water and poured it over the dogs and they quit fighting. Mother gave me a dollar and sent me with George to the doctor. The doctor cleaned up the hand, put some yellow salve on it and wrapped it up.

It was not long after this that someone poisoned Rover. Oh, how I cried! Even Art [her future husband] cried. We laid Rover in a box, put some cloth over him and nailed a cover over it. Then we buried our dog. Art was the minister. I don't recall what he said, but it most likely was not good because we thought we knew who poisoned our Rover. We even picked flowers and put them on the grave.

Lena L. Borchardt, about 1900

MAUDE BAUMANN, AGE FIFTEEN, IN HER JOURNAL ABOUT HER FAMILY'S COVERED-WAGON TRIP IN 1900: "I CAN'T HARDLY WRITE ON ACCOUNT OF THE MOSQUITOES. THEY'RE BIGGER THAN ELEPHANTS."

We did not plan family picnics [in the early 1900s]. Since the children carried lunch to school and to the men working in the fields in summer, the family preferred to eat in the dining room away from the flies and mosquitoes that were prevalent outdoors. This was before the use of chemicals to control pests.

Agnes Mary Kolshorn, early 1900s

We once had a cage full of field mice. Eldest brother Fred was always on the lookout for a nature lesson for his young sisters. The first summer, the long grass was scythed and stacked and immediately became home to the field mice. So the boys built a large screened cage and set it out back of the house at the edge of the east bank.

Then we surrounded a haystack, one with pitchfork and the others with gunnysacks. At a signal, the pitchfork man lifted the hay and whee! Out darted the little mice. We were supposed to pounce and catch the little grey things with our gunnysacks. I suspect that I, being a timid sort, let the others do most of the pouncing. However, enough were caught to start a collection in our cage. There was grass on the bottom, deep enough to hide

Now here's a big pet! Or, more likely, the horse belonged to a traveling photographer who knew how to entice parents to part with some cash. We know little of the subjects, but the educated guess is it's a Northfield scene in about 1900. Ride 'em, cowkids.

them when they wanted. What we fed them, I don't recall, but we did watch them, fascinated.

All was not serene in that cage. There were fights and personality clashes … These little creatures met a sad fate at summer's end. The boys were told to carry the cage down to the lake and drown them. I'm sure they didn't enjoy that. But the project was successful from our viewpoint. We learned that field mice are pretty, clean little creatures, and we lost all fear of them. And that mice have personality problems too.

Isabel Shephard Tryon Thibault, 1910s

I started riding a horse about the same age as I started milking, six. Dad threw me up on the back of a horse—a big one. It wasn't like those Clydesdales you see on the Budweiser commercial—it was a lighter horse, but still a heavy worker. There was actually a team—Barney and George. I remember going up and down the tallest one, Barney. Oh, I liked that! I rode on a western saddle, but by the time I was twelve or thirteen years old, I'd just jump up on him bareback!

I always felt close to horses. I used to just lean up against them. Did you know that when you do that, if a horse wrinkles his nose, he likes you? Horses would wrinkle their noses and put them up against me. I'd greet them.

Nellie Stone Johnson, 1911

She went on to fight for equal pay for women in the late 1930s and was the first black woman appointed to office in Minneapolis.

Children at a mission,
Redwood Falls, with
their sweet shaggy dog,
about 1940

*Betty Powell, of Irish and Ojibwe descent, was raised in the traditional ways of
her Ojibwe grandmother along the wilderness of the Minnesota-Ontario border.*

The animals were my playmates when I was growing up. My grandma and
grandpa always let us have wild things to tame if they were orphaned. I
guess I tamed about everything there was to tame. I still can't understand
how my grandpa, grandma and mother put up with me. Anything that was
orphaned, I took care of.

We had a little otter that I loved so much, and I still think of him every
time I see an otter track. He used to cuddle around my neck and dig in my
pockets. He would go down and play in the little creek that ran close to our
home. He would go to this little river to hunt and fish. Then he would come
back into the house and dry off.

We also had a little beaver later on in my life. I have forgotten where we
got this little beaver but I remember, just as plain as yesterday, when it used
to live in the house with us. It was more like a cat because it never made a
mess inside. She always made her wants known and went outside. Every
time the wind blew she would try and plug up the holes that sometimes
develop in a log cabin. She lived one whole winter with us but died in the
spring. There was a doctor visiting us, and he did an autopsy. He thought she
probably ate too much bannock [pan-fried bread] and her digestive system
failed to work properly.

Betty Powell Skoog, 1930s

Time for Gardner Reynolds to take a snooze with his dog, Juno, as his pillow in about 1895. Gardner's dad, Myron Reynolds, was a veterinary professor at the University of Minnesota. The family lived in St. Paul's St. Anthony Park neighborhood, near the farm campus.

The Dunn children of St. Paul knew in about 1910 that bunnies make good pets, too.

A summer day on the porch in about 1910. The woman and girl dressed up for the photo, pulled out a worn carpet and pillows to the porch, and invited the pooch to participate.

The Christmas I remember most was when we ate Petrice, our goose. She had come to our farm [near Aurora] as a gosling. Thinking she was a gander, we named her Pete. When she laid an egg, we renamed her Petrice. She thought she was human and would have nothing to do with the other fowl. She always followed me around the farm, daffy, crooning to me, and I could never sit down without her getting into my lap and resting her head on my neck. She also wanted to mother puppies, and when our cocker bitch, Flicka, left her babes unattended once, Petrice nestled on them, wings outspread, crazy eyes soft and maternal. What a hooha there was when Flicka discovered Petrice gabbling there. The puppies didn't mind, but Flicka

You know the theory that people and their pets tend to look alike after a while? This was Northfield in about 1890.

went mad. Foaming at the mouth, she attacked. Petrice did her best to fly, but, weighing twenty pounds, all she could do was lollop away, flapping her wings, while Flicka helped her along by grabbing mouthfuls of rump and feathers . . . At last, poor Petrice ran headlong for the doghouse and stuck fast in the doorway, her fanny exposed, her cries dreadful, as Flicka lay down and promptly began denuding that plump backside. I scolded Flicka away and pityingly hauled Petrice feetfirst out of the doghouse. And when Christmas came and Petrice lay wreathed with parsley on the platter, I could not touch a drumstick or lay a fork on her white meat. I could not eat at all; cranberry sauce sparkled, sweet potatoes swam in golden sauce, apple pie bubbled and crisped, all to no avail, as I sat, pea green, at the table, poised on the edge of my chair, the brittle tears ready to break down my face.

Shirley Schoonover, 1940s

At least the dog didn't have to dress up for the Fergus Falls photo shoot of Hans Hanson's son in about 1900. Unfortunately, names of the boy and dog weren't recorded with the picture.

Challenges

In all of time, childhood has not been kind to many, if not most. Poverty, neglect, and crime were no strangers in Minnesota. Orphan trains brought in children, yet many were chosen only to provide cheap labor. A sixteen-year-old farm boy, smitten with stories of the Jesse James gang, murdered for the fun of it. Sometimes kids must grow up too quickly.

Social Agencies

Following the terrible arraignment of the public dance hall from Judge Grier N. Orr of Saint Paul, the head of the juvenile court, an ex-police judge and an authority exceptionally competent to speak, the law enforcement league has taken steps which it is believed will put such places out of business. Judge Orr says that his long years of experience in the court convince him that not even the wine rooms of disreputable saloons work as much ruin and woe as do the indiscriminate public dances.

"I am not opposed to dancing," said Judge Orr, "but I am violently opposed to certain kind of public dance halls. There is more evil, more infamy, more shame, and a greater number of hopelessly wrecked lives resulting from such places than from the shameful winerooms which are a blot on the name of so many American cities."

"Take the boys into partnership" and the girls too, Judge Orr advises. He ascribes many a boy and girl gone wrong to the carelessness of parents, and too little friendly parental fellowship and interest. "Every man should so live that in his pleasures and amusements, he can take his boy with him," the judge said. "Do that, and the boy's salvation is assured."

Minneapolis Humane Society,
citing an unnamed newspaper, March 5, 1908

The public became concerned about poor treatment of children and of animals at about the same time. That's why the Minneapolis Humane Society, organized in 1883, was founded and conducted for the prevention of cruelty to not only animals but children, too. And there was much cruelty to consider. The files are chock-full of numbing cases. Names are withheld for privacy considerations from the following 1916 case.

With tailoring scissors nearly as big as she, a girl worked on a paper project at the Unity Settlement House in Minneapolis, in roughly 1925. The agency was sponsored by the Church of the Redeemer, now First Universalist Church of Minneapolis.

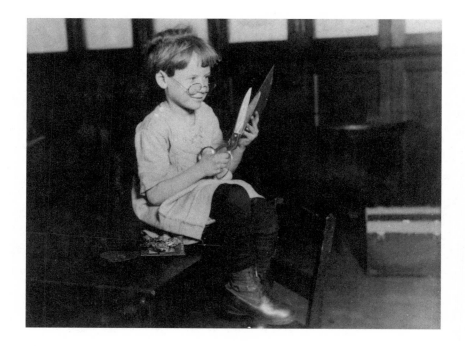

Statement of complaint: Father away all day, works part of the time, mother goes to neighbors or show, leaves children alone three to five hours at a time.

2/11/16. [Humane Society agent] called, found children [three boys, ages 5, 4 and 2] in house alone, house filthy from top to bottom. Children had taken kerosene out of lamps and were playing around stove with kerosene all over the house, even upstairs. All very dirty and scantily clad, [the 2-year-old] having practically nothing on. All the children were extremely dirty, looking as tho they had not been washed for days. One bed upstairs in which entire family sleeps. Shed attached to house, with door from house opening into same, as dirty as the house. Called in two neighbors to witness conditions. After being there about one hour, [the mother] returned, says she has heart trouble and cannot do much work. Question this. Says they moved here from [a northern Minnesota city] last August, does not know where [husband] is working, and was inclined to be uncommunicative. Neighbor says children often are seen in the back yard, even in the coldest weather, lightly clothed and dirty. Says [mother] leaves them often.

2/14/16. Called, no one at home, in a short time [mother] came with the three children, house a little cleaner and some food in the kitchen. [Mother] says they can get along now, but I think this family should be constantly watched. [Mother] says [father] working last three days, but [neighbor] says he saw him at 11 A.M. today.

2/15/16. Phoned University Hospital. [Mother] made about half a dozen visits to see doctor between November and Jan. 15th. Diagnosed suffering from stomach trouble, but no chronic heart disease. Dr. slightly disposed to think some mental trouble is present.

2/23/16. Phoned [neighbor] who said she had gone into the home, found children alone playing with broken glass, fire in the stove and house quite dirty, very little to eat in the kitchen.

3/14/16. [Mother] says [father] is working today, says she is unable to do much with her work and sends her wash to the laundry. Neighbor who lives across the street told me she had sent [mother's] wash to the laundry and paid for it. Grocer says [father] has not paid him anything since 2/25/16 when he made his first and only payment. Says he cannot give them much more credit and will notify us if he stops.

3/21/16. Stopped at grocery and found he had stopped credit.

6/20/16. Visited home, found no one in but filthiest condition existed. Floors were black with dirt, food was spilled on kitchen floor, dishes dirty on table, chairs covered with clothing and clothing scattered around. Milk spilled all around. The space immediately outside the back door seemed to have been used as a slop pile. Visited some neighbors who claimed that the family was getting along tolerably well now.

Minneapolis Humane Society records

This photo was labeled "Children's activities." It was shot at the Volunteers of America Rest Camp, North Oaks, on railroad tycoon James J. Hill's country estate in about 1920. Restful, hmm?

Betty is 15. She spent last summer washing dishes in a steamy city restaurant. That is, except for her vacation. When Betty arrived at the Big Sisters' summer camp on Lake Minnetonka, she was a sorry sight—a little girl already crushed by a world of grown-ups.

Then a remarkable thing happened. Overnight Betty became a camp leader. Before her vacation was over, many younger girls sought her out for advice and help and companionship. Betty went back to her job refreshed as though from a North Cape cruise.

How long was Betty's vacation? One short week.

Mary breezed through high school at the top of her class. But she had no intention of stopping her education there—even though the money did stop. All her young life she's had one burning ambition—to take a certain college course.

So she applied to the Big Sisters for a scholarship. Every kind of test they gave her said go ahead.

Today Mary is a sophomore at the University of Minnesota, getting As and Bs in subjects few girls dare choose. She still has a long, tough way to go before her dream career comes true, but she'll make it.

You see, Mary's going to be a doctor.

"Little Stories about Little Sisters,"
Big Sister Association of Minneapolis, 1945

[There was an] unmarried young psychologist who was wont to lecture on "Five Laws for Raising Children." In the course of time, he went the way of all flesh and took unto himself a wife. Eventually came a child. Time passed, and the young psychologist changed the title of the lecture to "Five Rules for Raising Children." By and by, a second child appeared. After a further lapse of time, the title of the lecture became "Five Suggestions for Raising Children." Later a third child came. Then the lecture was on "Five Hints for Raising Children." After the advent of the fourth child, the child psychologist gave up lecturing.

Judge Gustavus Loevinger,
Big Brothers of Minneapolis annual meeting, 1950

BIG BROTHERS OF MINNEAPOLIS MOTTO, 1949: "WHEN GOD MADE MAN, HE MADE THE WORLD SIGNIFICANT; WHEN HE MADE A BOY, HE MADE THE WORLD INTERESTING."

Clara and Mary Radintz, three and four years old and born in Wayzata, were taken from their home, where they were neglected and abused, and admitted to the State Public School on August 17, 1892.

The same girls eight years later, on July 12, 1900, after successful adoption

Orphans

A little orphan girl, six weeks old, of German parentage, can be had for adoption. Inquire of Charles Lamby, cor. Main Street and Seventh Avenue, East Division.

Minneapolis Tribune, June 20, 1875

Orphan trains carried 3,500 children a year westbound from New York City in the early 1880s. Not all were orphans; slums in the East held people so poor and desperate that they gave up their children. Relatively few came to Minnesota— only about 340 in the three years before 1884. In that period, Michigan took in about 4,000, Illinois, 5,000, and Indiana, 6,000. The goal was to remove children from places where opportunities were few and immoral influences rampant and to place them in good, Christian homes.

Yet, there were enough rumors and bad outcomes that Minnesotans wondered if the system needed fixing. The Reverend Hasting H. Hart, head of the State Board of Corrections and Charities and formerly a Congregational pastor in Worthington, investigated in 1884. He concluded that it was not true that many "vicious and depraved" children were sent out by the Children's Aid Society of New York City, nor that a large proportion turn out badly, "swelling the ranks of pauperism and crime."

Hart did, however, decide that children unfortunately were hastily placed in homes without proper study. He recorded how the children were distributed:

The plan is as follows: A representative of the society first visits the town where distribution is to be made, and secures three leading citizens to act as a volunteer committee, pass upon applications for children, and take general charge of the matter. A notice is published in local newspapers inviting applications and announcing the day of arrival and distribution. I was myself a witness of the distribution of forty children in Nobles County, Minnesota [where Worthington is the county seat], by my honored friend, Agent James Mathews. The children arrived at about half-past three P.M. and were taken directly from the train to the court-house, where a large crowd was gathered. Mr. Mathews set the children, one by one, before the company, and, in his stentorian voice, gave a brief account of each. Applicants for children were then admitted in order behind the railing, and rapidly made their selections. Then, if the child gave assent, the bargain was concluded on the spot.

It was a pathetic sight, not soon to be forgotten, to see those children and young people, weary, travel-stained, confused by the excitement and the unwonted surroundings, peering into those strange faces and trying to choose wisely for themselves. And it was surprising how many happy selections were made under such circumstances. In a little more than three hours, nearly all of those forty children were disposed of. Some [adults] who had not previously applied selected children. There was little time for consultation, and refusal would be embarrassing; and I know that the committee consented to some assignments against their better judgment. There was similar speed in Freeborn, Rock, and Watonwan Counties, and, I presume, elsewhere. In Watonwan County, only six days intervened between the published notice and the arrival of the children, leaving no time for investigations by the committee. The committee usually consists of a minister, an editor, and a doctor, a lawyer or a business man. The merchant dislikes to offend a customer, or the doctor a patient; and the minister fears to have it thought that his refusal is because the applicant does not belong to his church. Thus, unsuitable applications sometimes succeed . . .

The evil is aggravated by the fact that, while the younger children are taken from motives of benevolence and uniformly well treated, the older ones are, in the majority of cases, taken from motives of profit, and are expected to earn their way from the start. The farmers in those counties are very poor . . . To my personal knowledge, some of [the children] were taken by men who lived in shanties and could not clothe their own children decently. A little girl in Rock County was taken by a family living on a dirt floor in filth worthy of an Italian tenement house. A boy in Nobles County was taken by a family whose children had been clothed by the ladies of my church, so they could go to Sunday School. I have seen other similar instances. Probably as many failures have resulted from unsuitable homes as from the fault of the

Waifs waited in the Humane Society office on December 23, 1914, in the era when humane societies served children—as well as animals—in need. The sacks of potatoes were ready for Christmas distribution. The oversized clothes must have been welcome gifts, too.

children. We believe the society should employ responsible, paid agents to investigate deliberately all applications beforehand . . .

The employer [who takes in a child] gives no security for redeeming his promises, and may discharge the child without warning "if found useless or otherwise unsatisfactory." A prosperous farmer in Watonwan County worked a boy all summer, and turned him out ragged just before winter, apparently to save board. He found him "useless," and there was no remedy. Employers agree to "treat them as their own in the matter of schooling," but many do not send their own to school.

In his 1884 report, Hart concluded that the Children's Aid Society should not send out children older than twelve. Teenagers had trouble adjusting to a new family, and most were taken only to provide cheap labor.

Some did find loving homes. Hart wrote, "Our examination shows, with reference to the children under the age of thirteen years old, that nine-tenths remain [don't run away or go home], four-fifths are doing well, and all incorrigibles are cared for by the society."

By the time orphan trains ceased to run in 1929, about 250,000 children from New York City and other eastern cities were relocated to rural homes, most in the Midwest, including about 4,000 in Minnesota. Some historians think that fewer than half were orphans; as many as a quarter had two living parents who couldn't or wouldn't raise them. Few were actually adopted by the families in which they were placed.

The Children's Home Society of Minnesota started as an orphanage, taking many of the children not chosen at train depots.

*   *   *

1918 newspaper ad:

> FOR ADOPTION: Catholic family only, bright, handsome, strong and healthy children. For particulars address E. J. O'Shea, Hastings hotel, Hawthorne av. and 12th st., Minneapolis, Minn.

The Minnesota Public Welfare Department sent Mr. O'Shea a scolding letter.

> The State Board of Control is very much opposed to public advertisement in connection with such matters. I should be glad to consider the subject with you in person at any time that you care to come to my office.

*   *   *

Mama told me at an early age that I was not her natural-born child, and that this meant I was a chosen child, "Not just an accident, like so many children who are with their natural parents." This was an opinion that I shared freely with my peers when I was losing an argument with them. It also had a positive effect on my childhood.

The situation was not an unusual one in our [St. Paul African American] community, where many people like Mama and Daddy took care of "abandoned" children. I knew quite a few chosen children. Some were "abandoned" to a friend or relative by their natural parents during those depression years where there wasn't enough chicken in the pot to feed all of the family. Some were "abandoned" by parents who lived in the South to relatives who lived in the North where life was more generous. Like myself, some were "abandoned" to families who didn't have children by young girls who got in trouble; and, of course, the high death rate produced its share of orphans, who were raised by Big Mama (usually the maternal grandmother). Many of these orphans were nurtured and wanted by people who could never have passed the test for adoptive parents. Although most of the children in the neighborhood were raised by both natural parents, those of us who were chosen children were raised with pride and dignity.

Evelyn Fairbanks, 1930s

Crime

When I was 5, Brother Willie was born, and Mother was sick for three months afterward. Orson and I stayed with Grandmother much of the time . . . One day a peddler came to the house. Of course, I was on hand to see what he had in his pack. He made big eyes at me and asked me if I knew what made his stomach so big. Then he said it was because he ate little girls just like me. I ran into the house and wouldn't come out again while he was there. For years afterward, I was afraid of peddlers.

Alice Mendenhall George, 1859

[St. Paul] is infested by a considerable number of little boys who appear to have nothing else to do except to waylay in pairs any decently dressed, well-behaved boy. The better dressed the boy, the more sure he is of being beaten and bruised by those good for nothing little ruffians. Yesterday afternoon a little boy was going up Wabasha street in a quiet manner, and was suddenly, and unexpectedly, assaulted by three rough boys. He received two or three blows in the face, and considerable blood flowed from his nose in consequence thereof. As soon as the boys struck their victim, all fled as fast as their legs could carry them around the corner into Third street. The attack was a piece of pure wantonness. It is a great pity that some of these little bruisers cannot be arrested and punished.

St. Paul Daily Pioneer, January 11, 1874

Two nice (?) young men—whose names are withheld out of deference to their parents—were arrested by officer West Sunday evening upon the charge of disturbing divine services. Flirting and unmannerly conduct will no longer be tolerated and as the churches have united in this matter of discipline, a reform may be looked for.

Minneapolis Tribune, October 26, 1875

The people of Taylor's Falls who have orchards are obliged to build fences around them sixteen feet high in order to keep the bad boys of that place from stealing the fruit.

Stillwater Gazette, May 10, 1876

Some time ago a Mrs. Storms, the wife of a mulatto man, living near the First Presbyterian Church, in lower town, gave birth to twins, and, in seeking for help, Mr. Storms succeeded in securing the services of a little white girl, seventeen or eighteen years old, whose duty it was to help take care of the twins, and do such other light work as is usual on such occasions. Mr. Storms, so far as anything of him is known to the writer, is regarded as a bright, intelligent man, of good character. He is at present, and has been for a long time, in charge of the sleeping cars on the St. Paul & Sioux City [rail]road.

Mr. Storms states that during his absence from home, and while attending to his legitimate business, a police officer named Nigand entered his house, and without any warrant or other paper authorizing him to do so, arrested the little girl and took her away; that the girl was subsequently taken before the municipal court, where she was tried upon a complaint charging her with being a vagrant, that is, an idle person without any visible means of support; that she was found guilty and sentenced to thirty days in the House of the Good Shepherd.

Yesterday morning, as soon as he found out about the matter, Mr. Storms and his wife rode up to the police headquarters for the purpose of ascertaining how it is that a police officer arrests a person who is committing no crime, without a warrant of arrest. They also want to know how it is that a person that is working for another, and being paid for that work, and who has a place to sleep and eat, and who pays for the sleeping and eating, can be arrested for vagrancy, tried for vagrancy, convicted for vagrancy, and punished for vagrancy. To Mr. Storms' untutored mind, this proceeding seems quite despotic and indefensible, and if the facts are as he states them, people will generally agree with him.

St. Paul and Minneapolis Pioneer Press and Tribune,
May 26, 1876

These boys were in the first *Minneapolis Journal* Newsboys' Club, about 1882. Life was tough for many poor newspaper carriers, known as *newsies*.

It is something to watch the antics of the newsboys that congregate around the east end of City Hall just before The Tribune appears. Last evening one of them challenged another to tussle in the fistic [boxing] arena. They adjourned to an alley nearby, and in about three seconds the boy that sent the challenge was the worst whipped youngster that has been seen in these parts lately. The one who got the worst of it was the largest of the two, and he is the little fellow's best friend now.

Some of the bootblacks have resorted to a sharp trick to-day. Two of them would approach a young man evidently from the rural districts and request that they be allowed to each black [polish] a boot, just to see who could do it the best, you know. Verdant [the "green" country boy] is afraid some game may be played on him, but at last agrees, and the boots receive a shine that the rural representative can see his face in. Then the boys demand payment and will not leave till they receive it. The granger grows very angry, but when one of the bootblacks inform him that they will inform the Mayor and have the police department out in full force, he reluctantly complies with their request, and they go around the corner and divide the spoils.

Minneapolis Tribune, July 25, 1876

Northfield became known across the nation when townspeople foiled the plans of a notorious gang of bank robbers, headed by Jesse James, on September 7, 1876. Two outlaws were left dead on the street, and the bank's bookkeeper was killed for refusing to open the vault (which turned out not to have been locked at all). Charles Armstrong was a boy when the robbery occurred near him, and in 1945 he wrote his recollections:

I was an orphan boy of nine years, living with relatives on a farm, three miles east of the town of Madelia. The news of the raid on the Bank at Northfield, the killing of the Cashier and the escape of the gang quickly spread, and I can remember vividly how terrified my sister, four years older, and I were because at the time we were alone on the farm and knew the robbers were being hunted.

At night we huddled together in a big chair fearing at every noise (once the prop under a window fell down) that the wicked men were at the door seeking shelter and meaning harm to us children. The family returned and the hunt for the fugitives continued several days . . .

I was herding the farmer's cows about a quarter of a mile from Madelia and I heard the train that I called "the four o'clock" go through. That was my signal to collect the cows and start for home. In a short time I heard the train backing up to the station and I hurriedly turned the cows into an enclosure and ran to see what had happened. A team and wagon with a double box and the end-gate out was backed up to the platform and men were bringing out the body of Charlie Pitts and putting it in the wagon, then came the three Youngers [Cole, Jim, and Bob] and Sheriff Glispin. The armed posse stood around the wagon. As the wagon started towards the town ¼ mile from the station, boys like I followed. Jim Younger who had been shot in the chin and was bleeding badly, had his face over the wagon side. When we passed one house, a woman hurried to the wagon and gave him a white handkerchief which he held to his chin. I went back to my cows and drove them two miles home and told my story.

The next morning the farmer told me to leave the cows in the barnyard, that we were all going to Madelia to see what further had happened. We drove in the lumber wagon. We were told the prisoners were guarded in the [Flanders] Hotel and the body of Charlie Pitts was in the very small jail and the door open so any who chose could go in and see the body, which we did. He was lying on a rough table covered with a sheet, and a sheet over him to his waist leaving his chest bare, the bullet hole plainly visible.

A sixteen-year-old farm boy near Perham loved reading cheap novels about such outlaws as the James gang and the Younger brothers, and that's why he went bad, or so the press said at the time.

In the spring of 1882, John Tribbitts "murdered in cold blood a surveyor and his assistant, rifled them of their watches and money, bought a new suit of clothes with a part of the cash and struck out for Montana to join the Cowboys," the Fergus Fall Journal *reported.*

The murdered men had been boarding at the Tribbitts house while they examined pine-covered lands about twenty miles east of Detroit Lakes. On about May 28, young John shot the surveyor in the back of the head, slit the assistant's neck with a knife, and finished him off with a hatchet. Then John (aka the "youthful desperado" and the "boy ruffian") hightailed it west, with the Perham constable on his trail. Arrested on the Missouri River where he had signed on as a ferry deckhand, John at first denied the crimes but soon gave it up.

Evidence strongly pointed to him at the preliminary hearing, and he was held in the Perham jail. He told a deputy and the surveyor's brother that he was inspired by reading dime novels about the exploits of the notorious Jesse James. When he stumbled upon the two surveyors and saw one sitting beside a marsh looking at a land plat, he said, "I just thought of pictures I had seen in the magazines of men being killed in that position, and I drew my shotgun to my shoulder and shot him through the back of the head. He never got up."

At 1 AM the following night, a band of about twenty armed and masked men surrounded the jail, battered down the door, and seized John. The surveyor's brother put the noose around his neck. The boy struggled and screamed for his

This little slugger in knickers was at a Salvation Army camp in about 1925.

father, who was at the jail. "Give me my gun, and I will give them hell to the finish," he yelled. Then he begged for his life, but no one was listening. The mob dragged him to the railroad track and flung up a ladder against a telephone pole, right in front of the sheriff's house. Within minutes, "the boy murderer of Perham" was dangling in the air. The lynch mob quickly dispersed.

The next morning as the Northern Pacific train neared Perham, passengers witnessed a remarkable sight—the dangling body of John Tribbitts, his ghastly face turned toward the train.

An inquest concluded, "Died from strangulation at the hands of parties unknown."

Otter Tail County Historical Society and the
Fergus Falls Journal, June 8–22, 1882;
Tribbitts's name was spelled variously as Trivits, Tribbets, and Trivitt.
The death certificate states "Tribbitts."

Italian boys from the Upper Levee in St. Paul made up this basketball team in about 1936.

During the Depression, a Ramsey County probation officer kept a diary of his work with a gang of boys, ages twelve to seventeen, who were known as the Ramsey Midgets. They had gotten into trouble for petty theft, smoking, playing crap games, and "rolling drunks." The probation officer directed the boys into YMCA-sponsored activities and worked with the courts and police on the boys' behalf. For reason of privacy rules, the names of the not-so-innocent have been changed here. (Their nicknames and place names remain as recorded.) Even the name of the hardworking probation officer must remain confidential.

1–8–32. Johnny called at the office, saying, "We've got the gang together and have organized a team. We were practicing at the Jefferson school but got kicked out because some of the kids were supposed to have stolen tennis shoes. Now we are going to meet in the John Marshall Junior High School gym on Fridays. We want you to be our coach if you will."

I called at the Marshall gym at 7:00 P.M. with Ray, 16 years old, and Bill, 16, who are to be acting coach and assistant, respectively . . . Eight boys were present tonight.

1–15–32. Stanley joined the gang tonight and added variety to the program by attempting to use the bubble fountain in the gym for a latrine, being stopped by Art. He also attempted to "lift" a watch on a filling station operator on the way home. Jerry and Mike are other new players, though Jerry is rather small for basketball, being only 54 inches tall, weighing 75 pounds. Jerry is somewhat noted for his frequent sprees after he has become drunk on beer. Both he and Stanley seem willing to do any sort of crazy thing the rest may suggest. Incidentally, Stanley is afraid of Jerry, though the former is much the bigger.

Art, Elmer and I talked about the team for a while after meeting tonight. The former two wanted to kick Stanley off the team because "he steals *all* the time," but finally agreed to give him another chance as long as he is so anxious to remain on the team.

1–22–32. Eleven fellows were present tonight. They worked like "nailers," but how can one stop them from smoking to and from basketball games?

1–29–32. Stanley was absent, thank goodness; everyone else present. I bawled out Art and Elmer about the smoking to and from meetings, told them I was not going to say anything about it, but did not want the gang to smoke while riding home with me (am driving them down to Ramsey Plgrd. after meetings as it is almost a mile and a half hike to the school) and want them to see smoking stops.

2–3–32. We played the scouts of Troop #72 at their meeting place on Roy and Shields streets, Bethlehem Lutheran Church. Our fellows played a clean game against great odds and succeeded in scoring 10 points to the other team's 12. The fellows are still smoking on the way home, though they did not smoke between halves anyway.

2–5–32. Played a team from Hazel park who came to our gym by truck tonight. The other fellows were as green as grass, so were beaten by us 26 to 0. Even our real midget, "Mosquito," (also known as "Dago"), played in spite of his 52 inches and barely 70 pounds . . .

Some of the gang started to kid about "Esther," bragging a little to each other about their escapade of last October when most of them had immoral relations with a girl in back of the Peoples Church. Both Art and I called them on the talk with a measure of success, I guess . . .

Neighborhood children in March 1964 surveyed the damage to a vandalized house in West Duluth. Someone was inside the front door: maybe a ghost buster? The house was rumored to harbor spirits.

3–3–32. It was decided that the case of Stanley should be referred to the Juvenile Court as otherwise he would continue getting in trouble. Tom, who is his best friend, said that Stanley can't keep from stealing and that they beat him too much at home . . .

3–4–32. Stanley appeared in Juvenile Court this afternoon and was placed at the County Boys' Farm School at Highwood, Minnesota, the Judge believing that the boy was not being properly supervised at home nor properly disciplined, that he needed a change of environment and more sympathy . . .

3–5–32. Called at the downtown YMCA this evening, found Tom, "Mosquito" and "Louse" shooting pool. They said it was too cold for the rest to come down. We left the "Y" at about 9:30, found a hamburger shop where I treated them to hamburgers and coffee. Each remembered to thank me when I let him off at home.

*   *   *

Dr. Lawrence M. Gould, president of Carleton college, Northfield, told members of Big Brothers, Inc., at the Curtis Hotel, "the words 'striptease' and 'sex appeal' are all too common among today's youth.

"Advertising, which commands the best and most expensive American talent and utilizes press, radio and movies, is not inherently bad, but has been generally reduced to ignoble purposes," he said.

"Our youngsters are the victims of an age without standards, and the atomic bomb or universal military training are not the real problems today. What we need is to instill into youth the realization of basic philosophical and spiritual beliefs."

Minneapolis Times, January 30, 1948

Seasons

FACING PAGE

Two girls in "swimming dresses" frolicked in the water one fine summer day in about 1900. Those woolen outfits were heavy when wet.

In Minnesota, we've always based our stories on the seasons. Life is framed by winter blizzards and summer camps, spring flowers and autumn gatherings. The games we play, the food we eat, the family and friends we see—it all matters whether it's June or November. And why are so many of our memories rooted in winter? Maybe because it's about eight months long.

Summer

Southerners, it was said in the 1880s, had one overriding ambition in the summertime—to escape the sweltering heat. It was on the cooler shores of Lake Minnetonka that some of the South's super-rich families chose to spend June, July and August. From the late 1870s through the early 1890s, they rode Mississippi River steamboats to the Twin Cities, then rode the 20 or 30 miles west to Lake Minnetonka on branch lines of railroads. At the peak of Minnetonka's "golden age"—1884—27 wooden hotels and boarding houses, scattered around the lake, catered to the whims of the wealthy. Most of the hotels were felled by fires.

A judge named Weatherby spent a boyhood summer in the 1880s at the Hotel St. Louis, one of the ritzy hotels. Weatherby later rhapsodized:

> You see, our family lived in northwest Mississippi, best cotton belt there is, plenty of rain in the winter and spring, but a sizzling inferno all summer. Great for cotton! But if you knew Mississippi summers, you'd know what Minnetonka and that fine hotel meant to our parboiled family. Why, I never struck anything as cool as that Hotel St. Louis. Some magic about that climate, too—it gave us appetites like yearlin' calves . . . Gulf fish? Shucks! Nothing like your bass and pike . . . Your nights up there beat everything. Many a night I've stood on one of those hotel verandas watching the moon rise—first brushing its light across the stars, then throwing it down on the lake in sheets of silver.

On a sultry Sunday in July 1890, a river steamer named the Sea Wing *set out on a pleasure excursion. About two hundred passengers and fifteen crew members were to take a leisurely, day-long trip on a lovely stretch of the Mississippi River into Lake Pepin. Attached to the boat was a barge for partying and dancing, with a four-piece band to furnish music. A crowd boarded at Red Wing. Among the passengers were families with teenagers and small children. Others were young couples hoping for a romantic trip.*

Instead, disaster. A fierce storm that evening tore up Lake City and roared on to Lake Pepin and the crowded steamer. The unwieldy Sea Wing *tipped to a 45-degree angle, balanced on its side for an instant, and then flipped over completely.*

More than one hundred passengers were trapped inside cabins. Others floundered in the water. Some tried to swim to shore. Winds, hail, and heavy rain tormented them. Girls and women—few of whom knew how to swim— were further hampered by ankle-length skirts. A survivor remembered seeing white dresses on the water's surface as the women struggled.

When the waters gave up the last of the dead a few days later, the official number was ninety-eight. Drowning was the main cause of death. The accident took a large toll of women and young girls; of the fifty-seven females thought to be on board, only a few survived. Searchers discovered Kate Schoeffler dead inside the cabin, clasping her infant son, Frederick, in her arms. No one had the heart to separate mother and son, and the two were carried to shore together, the St. Paul Pioneer Press *reported. "Men and women, boys and girls stood in groups discussing some new phase of the horror," the paper said.*

The captain, who survived, was blamed for setting out in a storm and for overloading the boat. His license to pilot steamers was temporarily revoked. His much greater hardship was losing his wife and eight-year-old son in the tragedy.

The Sea Wing *catastrophe is still ranked among the worst accidents on U.S. waters.*

*   *   *

I had no sister now [she had died of diphtheria], so played mostly with boys and we did have fun. We had a dugout. We dug a hole in the ground and covered it with boards. It was a shack. Here we roasted potatoes and apples in the fire. Did they taste good! But all black and charred on the outside. Some of the other children would come over, and we played "Run, sheep, run" "can-can" and "anti-anti-over." Anti-anti-over was one of our favorites. There were two teams, one on each side of the building. When the side that had the ball hollered "anti-anti-over!" and threw the ball over the roof and it was caught by someone on the other side, that person would try to catch someone from the opposite side. If all of the players were caught, the side with the ball won. If the ball was thrown and didn't make it over the roof, you had to yell "Pigstail" and throw again.

In the game of can-can, two holes, each big enough to hold the end of a bat, were dug about twenty feet apart. The two batters each held a bat in

Always a magnet for kids, families, and lovers, Minnehaha Falls drew appreciative children in about 1955.

the hole, facing each other. Two cans were placed about a foot behind the bat hole and about four inches apart. A player on the opposing team stood behind each batter and one rolled the ball, trying to knock over the cans on the other side. Each can knocked over was an out. Three outs and those who rolled the ball got the bats. The batters' job was to hit the ball so that they could run and change holes before their opponents could recover the ball and knock a can over. Each change of holes was a point and the game was won by scoring the first 21 points.

One Sunday Mother gave me one dollar so that my two brothers and I could go to Minnehaha Falls. We left quite early in the morning and took the streetcar. The fare was just five cents each. When we got there, we each had two hamburgers at five cents each. The boys had some merry-go-round rides. I didn't dare go on; I was afraid of getting sick. We walked down to the river and the boat landing, looked at all the animals [at the zoo] and had another hamburger. We saved just 15 cents for our ride home.

Lena L. Borchardt, about 1900

It is strange to me that I remember the house at the lake almost better than the town house [in Minneapolis] for we were only there three months each summer and in town the other nine. Our house out there [on Lake Minnetonka] was at Northwood as it was called for years. The name was later changed to Arcola . . . Our house was a comfortable, wooden affair with a large porch running the width of it in front, with swings and easy chairs where we practically lived. Inside there was a good-sized living room with the stairs leading directly out of it. I can see the bead curtains now, hanging between the living room and dining room—straws strung on threads with now and then a colored glass bead. How we children used to love to run through these curtains and feel the strings sort of drip over us like a shower of water. Between the dining room and the kitchen was a big porch stretching the full width of the house. This was called the summer kitchen, and it was a fascinating place for me. Here were the big ice boxes and long tables where all the good things were made . . . The granite milk pans were set out here for Mr. May, the milkman, to pour the milk out of his huge tin cans into ours and collect the tickets and tear them off . . . I remember once a minnow was found in the milk, and it wasn't surprising as Mr. May used to drive his milk truck into the lake and wash his cans by sloshing them around in the lake . . .

We had one of the first toilets and bath tubs at the lake, for Father was always fastidious about himself and did not like to rely on the lake for his bathing, as most of the lake dwellers did. Before that . . . the water had to be

Toes in the water, sun hats on some heads, sailboat ready to go: What could be sweeter than a summer day on a Minnesota lake? This was in about 1900.

heated in buckets and dumped in [a tub], so it was quite an event when we children had a real warm bath. We were only allowed in the lake three times a week and were timed to twenty minutes, and in August and September we could not go in at all. [It was considered unsanitary.]

Apparently there were no little girls at Arcola, for I spent my entire summer playing with boys. I never wore shoes or stockings except on rare occasions, and I can feel now that burning feeling of having to put on slippers when my feet had broadened out by being barefooted.

Margaret Jackson Bovey, about 1900

Guys in knickers at the Phyllis Wheatley Settlement House on Minneapolis's north side in about 1925 were either choosing teams or deciding who was up to bat. Settlement houses provided educational, recreational, and other social services, usually in inner cities. This one served African American families.

If Farview Park was a lively place in winter, it was even more so in summer. Then baseball was the thing. It was a regular event to get a game of "scrub" going. Or we chose up sides for team games. Since the park was only three blocks away, our Sixth Street bunch could hurry off to Farview at the drop of a suggestion. Lefty Cliff Borgen, who lived across from us, was a natural pitcher and began throwing when he was only eight or nine years old. He had a great curve that nowadays would be called a screwball, dipping away from a right-handed batter. From somewhere, a catcher's pad and mask turned up, and I was frequently found behind the plate in the receiver's spot. I did not like the bruised shins or stung fingers from foul tips, but I caught when no one else would, and usually no one else would.

Occasionally, "Rube" Schauer, a pitcher for the Minneapolis Millers who lived near the park, showed up at the Farview field to give us kids some pointers. I recall that I was catching one Saturday morning when Ol' Rube took the mound. I had never seen such a curve or drop before! The kid pitchers usually aimed for a spot and hoped. Rube was something else. I looked with awe as his curveball followed the end of the swinging bat in its arc. And the drop! It came toward the plate and then nosedived, so I had to scoop it out of the dirt. We were proud to have the big pro from the Millers show us how it was done.

Melvin Lynn Frank, 1910s

Boy Scouts camped at Pine Slough on the St. Croix River in about 1930. We can only hope that the mosquitoes didn't find their pup tent. Unlikely, huh?

SCOUTS LIKE TO CAMP? O BOY! AT PINE SLOUGH, ST. CROIX RIVER

One summer, my elder brother and one of his friends decided on a camping trip [near Lanesboro] to initiate our new 10x12-foot wall tent . . . A farmer gave us permission to pitch our tent on a grassy spot about four hundred feet from the barnyard and two hundred feet from the river . . . .

Following breakfast, we went over to the river to try our hands at fishing. After a couple of hours in the sun and with very little luck at angling, we returned to camp. As we approached the tent, we were horrified to see that we had some unexpected and unwelcome visitors. Although the barbed wire fence kept the cattle and horses away from the site, it formed no barrier for the half-dozen spring pigs that were cavorting into, out of and around the tent. They had gotten into our provision box and done some damage. But the most maddening and disgusting sight, with cannibalistic overtones, was that of the little pigs dragging our slab of bacon along the ground. We chased the pigs back to the barnyard, retrieved the bacon and buried it . . . Admittedly, we were lacking in experience and equipment; but somehow I never acquired a yen for camping out.

Gerhard A. Ellestad, 1910s

Looking for items to salvage—maybe the bike?—after a tornado tore through Anoka in about 1939

In 1925 we were victims of a tornado . . . It was evening and dark. We heard the rain come down and then saw the funnel cloud, and then there was sudden stillness, the vacuum of the cyclone cloud. My father had just come into the house after milking the cows, and we all made a dash for the "cellar," which was nothing but a hole in the ground under the house, about 10 by 8 feet, which we entered from the kitchen. We sat and shuddered as we heard objects crash all about us. It sounded like cannons going off. Water seeped into the cellar. After the noise abated, we cautiously lifted the trap door and saw that there was about an inch of rainwater covering the linoleum floor. Then we went outside and the barn was gone! Sections of the roof had been blown a half-block away. The sides of the barn were splintered and scattered all over like matchsticks. Strangely though, all 20 cows remained in their stanchions and chewed calmly on their cuds.

The next day we were all thankful to be alive. Unfortunately, two of our neighbors had been killed.

A few days later, my father assessed the damage and decided to rebuild . . . No architect was necessary as Mr. Hokenson [a carpenter] knew from memory how a barn was supposed to be built . . . He and my father agreed on the price, which was $500 for everything. The only problem was that the job took longer than it should have. Mr. Hokenson and his assistant were sober only about half the time.

Manuel Ruder

Dust storms were quite frequent and were a frightening thing to see, at least from a small child's perspective. When a dust storm moved into our area [Westport, in west-central Minnesota], you could see this huge black cloud of dust coming right at us. We always ran into the house when we saw this cloud coming. When the storm hit our farm, the sun would dim considerably and we would barely be able to see our barn, which was about 300 feet from our house. At times it would become so dark inside our house, we would light the lanterns to provide adequate light in the house. No one went out of the house during these storms unless it was absolutely necessary. My older brothers would place handkerchiefs over their nose and mouth in the event that they had to tend to the livestock. The little ones stayed put in the house.

I can remember being frightened by the darkness during supposedly daylight hours. You could hear the wind howling outside, and the dust and dirt blowing through the windows. During these storms, dust would get inside the house and cover everything in there.

After a storm ended, we would go outside and view the landscape. Dirt from the storm would drift into banks, much like a snowstorm, only not as large. Most of the fence on our farm eventually became buried by dirt banks. Tumbleweeds, which were plentiful, would roll with the wind and become hung up on the fences. The tumbleweeds would in turn catch the drifting dirt much like a snow fence does in the winter . . . Eventually the fences would become buried by the dirt, and we would be able to walk right over them. Livestock suffered terribly . . . They would eat just about anything, including thistles and even tumbleweeds.

Lawrence Schaub, 1930s

Good name for a camp: Fun in the Sun Day Camp, at St. Paul's Hallie Q. Brown Center, in the state's centennial year of 1958. The center was the equivalent of Minneapolis's Phyllis Wheatley House.

Our days began at 6:00 A.M. with a morning dip in the cold water of Snail Lake. In between meals, which began with the first few lines of "Praise God from Who All Blessings Flow," were scheduled crafts, sports, and, of course, Bible study. Dr. Crump came to the camp each year to give us a class on sex education, which consisted mostly of birth control (abstinence) and avoidance of venereal disease (abstinence).

Evelyn Fairbanks, late 1930s

What I remember most from my early years was summer. On summer nights, we would sit on the stoops of our houses and listen to the electric buzz of cicadas and the hubbub of other insects. Men would be on their after-dinner walks, speaking different European dialects of Yiddish. After the dinner dishes were done, women would start to straggle slowly out from their houses "to catch a breeze" and visit with neighbors. (There was no air-conditioning for us back then.) The evening would end with us being called in to our baths and bedtimes.

I remember trying to sleep at night with my head resting on the window ledge, hoping to feel a cool breeze. Outside, I would hear Dad watering the lawn by hand with a hose and kids playing baseball or hide and seek in the dark. I would try to feel some wind while listening to the cicadas and crickets talking. Nights seemed endless during some of those unbearable July and August heat waves.

Sandra Kreamer, 1940s

It's a whopper! These children were showing off their catch—a walleye?—near Detroit Lakes, in about 1943. It's said that the single most commonly photographed subject in the United States is a fisherperson and the catch. (Followed closely by kids in front of Christmas trees, with their holiday catch.)

Neal Freer, nine, of Moorhead, caught this fifteen-pound northern in Eagle Lake near Brainerd in 1967. He used a crappie hook on a fly rod. It took Neal and his dad, Robert, half an hour to land the thirty-six-inch beauty.

Long and lean, William Clark and James Hiemenz cooked their noon meal in a fire ring at a Works Progress Administration day camp near St. Cloud in about 1939.

It's funny, if in retrospect totally understandable, how we can remember smells of childhood, when the olfactory senses were birth-given sharp, before adult vices dulled them. The smells can be so specific and become so imbedded in our memories, recalling places and periods in our young lives. Like how the skunky-smelling iron-laced water from the faucet above the resort cabin sink, with its reddish brown stains ringing the porcelain edge of the drain, assaulted the nose each time I raised a glass to drink or smothered my face with a washrag. And the essence of decay that came with hauling up an anchor entangled with cabbage weeds and heavy with clumps of mud and muck from the lake's bottom. Long after the last marshmallow had been roasted, the night's breeze brought the acrid edge of the dying bonfire in through the screen window of the cabin.

William Albert Allard

Autumn

Even children routinely recorded the Minnesota weather.

Oct. 21, 1862

Today was Indian summer and extremely hazy and extremely, very extremely, very much extremely, very darned much extremely windy. I think the hardest wind I ever knew of. The 1st thing after I got to school was Ross coming in saying "A house on fire on the bottom." We went out and found Stringer's house in one perfect blaze. We ran down there and when we got there we found 2 stacks of hay and a woodpile (large) on fire. Afterwards a flat-bottomed boat caught on fire, but was hauled away and put out before it burned up. When I got there we all went into a shanty that was near and began to bring out things . . . I went in and took two or three boards and then thought it was more fun to look at the fire. Mrs. Stringer has a baby only 1 week old, and Mr. Stringer is up fighting the Indians [in the Dakota War]. The way it caught was they made too big a fire in the stove, and the stovepipe passed through the loft filled with corn husks and of course set fire to them. The wind blew Mr. Lasker's woodpile all to pieces scattering the boards down the bluff and everywhere. It took one board end over end over the lumber pile. And made me go right over the wood pile, came pretty close to lifting me.

Frederick Allis

In 1900 the Swiss women organized an auxiliary to the men's lodge, and they met on the first Friday of each month. Every November, around the 17th, the men would put on a "November Fest." The ladies would bring all the food, and the men brought beer and pop and a couple of hams. You could eat all you wanted and the cost was $1 per family. Then they danced and played cards. I remember that at one November Fest I drank 12 bottles of pop!

Lena L. Borchardt

Oct. 3, 1860

I went to the fair on the 26 of September. It was not as good as State Fairs generly are. There was a hog that weighed nearly 790 lbs. [Just for sake of

On Children's Day at the Minnesota State Fair in 1934, a boy tried out the kiddie merry-go-round. He looks manly enough to progress to the Tilt-a-Whirl or roller coaster.

comparison, the largest boar competition in the 1994 state fair featured a hog named Curt weighing 1,340 pounds.] And a miniature saw mill made by a boy 10 years old that would saw small logs.

Frederick Allis

Uncle, Aunty, Eva and I went by streetcar to the big State Fair. It was children's day, so everything for children was half fare. My uncle worked out a good system. He scouted around and found a good place to eat near where we came in. Then he told us girls we could go wherever we wanted, but when we thought it was noon, we should come to the eating place. So we ran around until noon, then went to eat "all you can eat for 25 cents"—beef roast, potatoes, bread, butter, sliced tomatoes and cucumbers and coffee or milk. After dinner we again went out scouting until supper. We all ate together again. Then we went up on Machinery Hill to watch the fireworks. Aunty's feet were so sore that she took her shoes off. When we were ready to go, her feet were so swollen that she had an awful time to get her shoes on again. Then on the way home on the streetcar, we were packed in like sardines and had to stand all the way home.

Lena L. Borchardt, about 1900

Fri. September 7, 1934. We went to the fair today. Bob Jewell and I climbed over the fence. A cop caught us. I got Jewell out of it. But I got stuck in Jail at 10 A.M. I got out of jail at 6 P.M. I didn't eat during that time. I ate seven hamburgers for supper.

William M. Cummings

The following all are from the 1934 and 1935 Minnesota State Fairs:

Three little farmers and their garden produce: cauliflower, sugar beet or yam, pumpkin.

Whoa! Squash that could squish this boy from Anoka County.

Hillcrest Count, a 1,900-pound bull and the University Farm's shorthorn entry, led by a ten-year-old boy.

A calf and his young owner. Looks like Elsie the Cow from the Borden ads, doesn't it?

Winter

It must have been difficult to find amusements and recreations for the winters in that fort [Snelling], so completely shut away from the world, and so environed by snow and ice, but various devices were planned to keep up the general cheerfulness and to ward off gloomy feelings and homesickness. I can dimly remember the acting of plays in which the gentlemen personated all the characters and the ladies and children looked on. I know the women of the plays [actually, men] looked very tall and angular, and there was much merriment about the costumes which were eked out to fit them. It may be that the performances were as much enjoyed as if everything had been more complete, for I know there was a great deal of fun and jollity at their theatricals.

Charlotte Ouisconsin Clark Van Cleve, 1820s

Babies in those days always slept in bed with their parents. It was considered a cruel thing to put a baby out of the parental bed, and perhaps it was. They had reason to fear the baby might freeze, the way homes were built in frontier days. Sometimes the snow would sift in around the windows. We often woke up with sheets all frosty around our noses.

Anna Lathrop Clary, 1860s

In the year 1873 I recall one of the saddest tragedies of Minnesota's pioneer history, the worst storm that has ever been experienced since white man came. This storm occurred in the month of January. It started suddenly of an afternoon, and in a short time completely overwhelmed the whole Northwest and continued with terrific fury for three days and nights. Many people who were entirely unprepared were caught and perished in vain attempts to reach shelter. About 300 persons lost their lives in that storm, and many hundreds were so badly frozen as to be crippled for life. One of our neighbors was caught out on the prairie in that storm and was within 20 rods of a settler's place, where he immediately collapsed. It was over a year before he could walk again without the aid of crutches, and I have often heard him tell, with tears streaming down his cheeks, of his frightful experience in that terrible storm. This man was the late Edwin E. Payne, in whose honor the town of Paynesville, Stearns County, was named.

A terrible blizzard it was, indeed, but not as bad as Walter F. Benjamin remembered. At least seventy people lost their lives in the storm, which took hold along the western border and southern half of the state.

*   *   *

Michael Dowling,
after he lost limbs in
an 1880 blizzard

*Another horrible blizzard swept through southwestern Minnesota in 1880,
with stinging winds and temperatures of nearly fifty below. Michael Dowling, a
fourteen-year-old farmhand and cattle herder near Canby, fell off the back of
a lumber wagon that day. Lost, he stumbled through blinding snow on the open
prairie. Eventually he came across a straw pile. He burrowed in, headfirst, and
there he spent the night.*

    *In the morning, Michael tried to stand but fell with a thump. His legs were
frozen, and when he tried to clap his hands, he said, "it was as if I had struck
two blocks of wood together." He managed to drag himself to a farmhouse.
Sixteen days later, without anesthesia, doctors amputated both his legs six
inches below the knees, his left arm below the elbow, and all the fingers and
part of the thumb on his right hand. With his mother deceased and his father*

absent, he was made a ward of Yellow Medicine County and lived in foster homes until 1883.

Give up? Not Michael Dowling. "I don't want to be pitied," he said. "I won't be an object of charity." Michael made a startling proposal to the county commissioners. If they would supply him with wooden limbs and pay his way for one year at Carleton College in Northfield, he would guarantee to take care of himself for the rest of his life. The board hesitated, then agreed.

Once he was fitted with two artificial feet and a hand, Michael acquired a college degree in a year, taught school, established a newspaper and a bank, owned several other businesses, served as mayor of Olivia and as a state legislator, married, and fathered three daughters. He traveled the world over in the cause of rehabilitation of the disabled, especially wounded World War I veterans. He told them, "From the neck down, a man is worth about $1.50 a day. From his neck up, he may be worth $100,000 a year."

He lived to age fifty-five in 1921, when he was felled by heart trouble. In his memory, the people of Minnesota raised $100,000 to build the Michael J. Dowling School for Crippled Children in Minneapolis.

* * *

The day before Christmas one year, Mother and my brother and I all went to my Aunt Maggie's for the day and did not return until after dark Christmas Eve. When we got up Christmas morning and went outdoors, there was a wonderful toboggan slide, built along the side of the stable! It was of lumber, with sides six inches or more high, and packed with snow and water until it was a glaze of ice. We went upstairs into the stable and out a small door onto a platform to start. We went down the slide, out the driveway and across the sidewalk, and when we learned how to steer better we could

Russell McMasters's children posed on a toboggan in St. Paul. The picture was taken in a photo studio, with a backdrop of a snowy scene and white stuff sprinkled on the kids' clothes. Outdoors that year—1886—the first Winter Carnival, with a magnificent ice palace, was held.

veer left as we reached the street and go sailing down the block. It was a wonderful Christmas gift from our dear stepfather. And of course we were all toboggan-minded that year because of the glorious Ice Palace in St. Paul, where we had gone several times with Mother and Ed and where we had had our first taste of tobogganing.

Blanche Stoddard Seely, about 1885

The great blizzard of 1888 occurred on a school day when I was 12 years old. I shall never forget it! The principal came into our schoolroom about 11 o'clock that morning. "Children," he said, and he sounded worried, "school is to be dismissed at once. I want each of you to go directly to your own home. Don't stop anywhere, and don't go to any other child's home."

By the time I had myself and my little brother encased in leggings, galoshes, coats, hoods, scarves and mittens, my stepfather [Ed] had arrived with the big two-seated sleigh. It was upholstered in deep red plush with large black swirls and it had huge red plumes, one at either side of the dashboard. And oh how lovely the sleighbells sounded! No automobile horn could ever give one the ecstatic joy that those jinglebells did.

Ed piled us in, together with as many more children as he could squeeze in, covered us all snugly with big buffalo robes, and as soon as he had delivered the first load he returned for more, meeting them at some distance from the school.

I don't know how my parents knew about the extreme danger of the storm (or how the principal did, for that matter) for there were no weather bulletins to be flashed through a radio and not even a telephone. I think most business houses had telephones by then, but neither we nor any of our friends had one. Had we stayed for the afternoon session at school, we could have had to stay there all night and probably for several days.

The blizzard was not quite so bad in Minneapolis as it was farther north. In Winnipeg, Manitoba, men were frozen to death between their houses and barns when they tried to get out to feed their stock.

Blanche Stoddard Seely

Being young on the north side [of Minneapolis] during the 1910–20 decade was such an adventure [that] there was never a dull moment, winter or summer. For one thing, we were close to Farview Park, which we usually called "Fairview" and which stretched in immensity for a small boy from Twenty-sixth Avenue North to Twenty-ninth and from Fourth Street to Lyndale Avenue. Within those dimensions was a world that encompassed ball diamonds, a playground with swings, a merry-go-round, teeter-totters, and all the rest. The park had picnic areas, tennis courts, hills for sledding and tobogganing, and a stone tower from which one could look out on what seemed to a child to be the whole city.

Smile if you're having
fun. These boys were
on the toboggan slide
at Groveland Park
Elementary School,
St. Paul, in 1961.

In winter the Farview hills were a constant challenge. One steep hillside was especially fearsome and bumpy for sliders—an awesome slope that gave breathtaking speed to a ride. Then when nature provided the white gift of snow, kids spent hour after hours on Flexible Flyers riding belly floppers till dark.

Of course, there was street sliding as well. The hill by the fire barn on Lowry was alluring. When it was icy, a youngster could go coasting for three blocks, all the way down to the Soo Line tracks by the shavings shed near the mill. This slide meant crossing the streetcar tracks on Washington Avenue. The boys walking back up the hill stood on the car tracks and signaled those at the top to come on when the coast was clear. Once in a while a boy would mistake a "don't come" signal for an "all clear"—like the day when a youngster went clean under a streetcar, right between the tracks, and continued for two more blocks, scared to death to the end of his ride. The rest of us were shaken, too, and must have been more careful after that experience. I cannot recall that any of the gang was hurt while sledding.

Melvin Lynn Frank

I remember winter in Duluth as heavy snowflakes falling silently day and night. Sometimes the snow pile would reach the second-story windows.

As a young child, these winter days were a comfort to me. I lived with my grandparents [Louis and Rachel Singer] and loved being in their kitchen. I especially recall one wintry afternoon, sitting with my grandfather playing dominoes while we watched a beautiful snowfall through the large kitchen window. We heard the cracking and snapping of the wood burning in the

Hail! Come on, guys, take cover. Downtown Duluth, 1898.

With help from her dog friend, a girl waited for a bite in an ice fishing contest at the St. Paul Winter Carnival in about 1955.

large black wood stove while Grandmother and her maid, Minnie, prepared dinner. The scent of roast chicken and homemade bread, mingled with the warmth from the wood stove, were too much for me. I fell asleep at the table, dominoes forgotten. Grandfather carried me to the daybed in the living room. When I awoke, dinner of roast chicken, mashed potatoes, salad and homemade lemon pie was the perfect complement to that winter day.

Charlotte Blizen, late 1920s

The water of Lake Owasso must have been well-regarded because, in the icehouse opposite my grandmother's cottage, huge slabs of ice that had been cut in winter were stored in sawdust and, in summer, sawed again, loaded on trucks and sold door-to-door for the ice boxes of those residents of St. Paul who lacked refrigeration.

Mostly the lake froze white or pale blue, but when it was best for skating it was at its most beautiful, a dark sapphire. We rode out through windswept patches, lured onward by the murmuring resonance beneath, until discretion suggested retreat to circling parents, siblings, aunts, uncles, cousins and friends near the warming fire on the shore.

Dorothy Snell (Tenenbaum) Curtis, 1930s

James L. Holman was bundled up on his sled in February 1897.

I was born fourteen months after [brother] Steve and three days after the worst snowstorm in Minnesota history—the famous Armistice Day blizzard of November 11, 1940—and I never heard the end of it. Every birthday after that, the recalling of that event took precedence over the anniversary of my own timely arrival. That old blizzard got fiercer and deeper; more stranded duck hunters and cars were lost every year afterward that it was remembered. Steve wasn't born after anything at all, so I suppose I wasn't too bad off at that.

The streets were barely cleared of the results of the blizzard for the trip to the hospital. As if that wasn't enough, as he drove down Hiawatha, Dad had to wait at Franklin for a train for what seemed like forever. Dr. Al was waiting when Mom arrived just in time to do what he was getting paid for.

Ronald C. Bradley at twenty-two months old was proclaimed the youngest curler in the world. With his child-sized "rock" in hand, he was at the Duluth Bonspiel (curling competition) in 1917. Curling is a team sport using heavy, polished granite stones and brooms. The Scots of Duluth were avid curlers and formed the Duluth Curling Club in 1891. There was even a Duluth curlers' song—with sixteen stanzas!

Ronald C. Bradley.
22 months old.
Youngest curler in the world.
Duluth Bonspiel, 1917.

Mom and I spent ten days at the hospital in room 315. This was the last real rest she was going to get for quite a while, a luxury that was costing us six dollars a day. Then we went home to 2509 33rd Avenue [Minneapolis].

Timothy Trent Blade

MINNESOTA OPTIMISM:

Talk about cold weather, it has been 35° and 40° below for a week, and when it is 25° we think it is warm enough to go out. But it seems a little warmer today.

Maude McGuire, February 5, 1893

Spring

For the first eight years of my life, Marjorie and I were strictly city children. Growing things were found only in rows, planted against fences or trailing out of metal urns . . .

But my first glimpse of wild flowers . . . and of woods where wild flowers grew came on a day in May, after we had just moved, that very week, to St. Anthony Park [in St. Paul]. That May noon day remains in memory as vividly as Wordsworth's vision of the daffodils did with him. But my vision was of mayflowers—so fairy-like.

Happy May Day. These Minneapolis schoolchildren in about 1940 had lovely May baskets—small containers of flowers or candies, left anonymously on friends' and neighbors' doorsteps.

Our maid Hilda led me across the street to a little dell behind the Harwood's house, and there were the flowers, a heavenly sight, to be picked and brought home . . . Every year after that, as long as we lived in the Park, on Mother's birthday, April 25, we arose very early, stealthily crept out of the house and hurried to the nearby woods to find a bouquet of Mayflowers to greet her at the breakfast table. Sometimes the spring was late, and there were none to be found. At least we could bring home a handful of moss or green leaves of the Mayflower plants.

Polly Bullard, about 1897

Mar. 26th 1911

It raind all last night and the grass looked greener than befor. It did a lot of good. It kept rainin till after none when all of a sodden it turned to snow. All afternone it was snowing. My but I am mad!

Glanville Smith

Muriel Prindle, about three, and her baby were out for spring air on the curb of a gravel street in 1896. They lived at 1605 East Second Street, Duluth.

Could it be spring? One of these five fellows had toes ready for warm mud. But he might have been rushing the season, as all Minnesotans are prone to do. Judging from the scene and the mud on their boots, they may have been cavorting in a factory district. Or maybe playing stickball in a muddy field.

Games and Toys

In the 1800s, store-bought dolls were a rarity. Boys and girls had handmade rag dolls. Most toys were meant for group play: kites, balls, marbles, jump ropes. Crayola introduced the first colored crayons for kids in 1903. Each box had eight colors—red, blue, yellow, green, purple, orange, brown, and black—and sold for a nickel.

"Backward! Turn backward, O Time, in thy flight;
Make me a child again, just for to-night."

Take me to my early home at Fort Snelling, and help me to live over again that happy time, when I knew nothing of care and sorrow, and when the sight of the dear old flag, run up each morning to the roll of the drum, and the sentinel's call each night, "All's well around," made me feel secure and at home, even in what was then a wilderness.

Charlotte Ouisconsin Clark Van Cleve, 1820s

Sept. 30, 1861

I went to Dan Rice's Circus on the night and afternoon. The principal feats were the Leap for Life, consisting of jumping off a high place near the top of the canvas and catching a rope hanging down about 20 feet off. Dan Rice with his blind horse who could understand almost every word spoken to him. A Rhinocerous, a kangaroo, a queer kind of a goat, two very small mules, who threw everybody who attempted to ride them.

Frederick Allis

Nice elephant, kid. This girl got a ride from a Shrine Circus beast in about 1931. Everybody, except the elephant, got to wear a hat.

Joseph A. Gilfillan's children posed with their pull toys in 1885. An Episcopal missionary on the White Earth Reservation, Gilfillan was known for his study of Ojibwe language and culture.

What boy would not be an Indian for a while when he thinks of the freest life in the world? This life was mine. Every day there was a real hunt. There was real game. Occasionally there was a medicine dance away off in the woods where no one could disturb us, in which the boys impersonated their elders, Brave Bull, Standing Elk, High Hawk, Medicine Bear, and the rest. They painted and imitated their fathers and grandfathers to the minutest detail, and accurately too, because they had seen the real thing all their lives.

We were not only good mimics but we were close students of nature. We studied the habits of animals just as you study your books. We watched the men of our people and represented them in our play; then learned to emulate them in our lives.

No people have a better use of their five senses than the children of the wilderness. We could smell as well as hear and see. We could feel and taste as well as we could see and hear. Nowhere has the memory been more fully developed than in the wild life, and I can still see wherein I owe much to my early training.

Of course I myself do not remember when I first saw the day, but my brothers have often recalled the event with much mirth; for it was a custom of the Sioux that when a boy was born his brother must plunge into the water, or roll in the snow naked if it was winter time; and if he was not big enough to do either of these himself, water was thrown on him. If the new-born had a sister, she must be immersed. The idea was that a warrior had come to camp, and the other children must display some act of hardihood.

Charles Eastman, 1860s

[I remember] the great search for Grandma's spectacles [eyeglasses]. She lost them and offered a reward of ten cents to any grandchild who could find them. We ransacked the house, even the sacred, darkened parlor, used only on the Sabbath and for weddings. I felt as awed in it as I would in a church. But not even here were the spectacles to be found. And nobody got that ten cents, for Grandma found them in the pocket of her Sunday dress. It was a terrible disappointment to lose the ten cents, because a dime looked as big to me in those days as a twenty-dollar gold piece would to my granddaughters.

Anna Lathrop Clary, 1860s

There were not many highlights or thrilling moments in our childhood [in Vasa]. We had to originate our own games, and as far as playthings were concerned, we HAD NONE. Neither did the neighbor children have them.

In another studio portrait, it was tea party time for a girl and her doll in 1908.

In about 1890, two girls and their dollies were ready for sleep in an iron bed. Why the bonnets? For warmth on a cold night, perhaps, on the second floor of a drafty farmhouse.

However, one Christmas evening, grandmother came in carrying some gifts for us four girls. She held them in her apron and tried to work up our curiosity for some minutes that seemed hours to us. One German porcelain doll for each of us! We were very excited to possess a doll! The porcelain head had such a pretty face! The dolls were all alike. There was no chance for arguments on whose was whose . . .

At the time, [my sister] Hanna began to make doll clothes (and she was very small when she started to work with her hands), she would cut into anything that looked shiny and pretty. She came across the pretty satin vest father wore as a groom. She invested her effort in it for doll clothes. Some time afterward, father asked me, what had become of his satin vest? I answered I thought it was hanging in the storeroom. He seemed satisfied with my answer, though the twinkle in his eye made me believe he was suspicious. When the ruin or fate of this precious apparel was discovered, Hanna was made to go to each grown-up to ask for forgiveness, but later she told me she never approached father.

Eva Tilderquist, mid-1870s

Who that has indulged to any extent in the fascinating game of croquet, or who has even watched the mode and manner of the various participators, old and young, has not witnessed instances of which the following is a reminder: Certain it is that a young girl never looks to better advantage than at croquet, on a smooth mown lawn, and surrounded with the usual appurtenances [trappings] of wealth. She always comes to the ground with a white dress of faultless freshness; hair falling on shoulders of that indescribable dewy coolness; skin of opaque whiteness; lips redolent of repose, and eyes downcast but wakeful. Old people now and then effect croquet, but they never look well. Matrons look best in the niche beside the domestic hearth. The moment she stirs from that, she is an unwelcome chronometer. Old gentlemen are generally too aldermanic in corporation to play the game, and when they attempt it, they look as much out of place as lace curtains in a canal boat cabin. They play with too much vim. Croquet is a game of languids, and some ennui, and these old pards play it as they would pole. If they make an error in favor of the opponent, they try to correct it by using unorthodox language, and pyrotechnical expletives of brag and banter. If that won't win, they jam the mallet in the grass and start for the house with a "darn such a game anyhow."

Stillwater Gazette, September 20, 1876

Marion Ramsey Furness in a letter to her daughter, Anita, regarding Anita's sister:

Jan. 5, 1896

Laura [age fourteen] is daft on the subject of skating. Talks, thinks and dreams about it all the time. Her ambition now is to be able to do the figure 8, the Dutch roll and the flying Mercury by spring. I believe she is getting on very well too.

*　　*　　*

From the back of our house, a well-worn path led diagonally across Raymond Ave. [in St. Paul] a block away from our street. This was the path we used to go to the stores near the Raymond Ave. bridge, and it led through more of the wooded area. This part of the woods . . . we children of Priscilla Street took over as our particular playground—wasn't it really an extension of our own back yards?

We each adopted as our own some one tree where we felt ourselves to be definitely at home. Here each of us had his own outdoor playthings—a pail or a pan, a kitchen spoon for sand and for digging, a stool or bench, perhaps a crude shelf nailed to the tree. Here we made mud pies, played store or school, or fashioned toys which played many parts in our "let's pretend" games from day to day. Often we ransacked the trash piles of the neighborhood, and we found treasures which we put to many uses. No children were ever busier than we, following the dictates of our very active imaginations.

This woodland playground, however, was not our only one. We all had grassy yards which opened in one continuous stretch near the street and into which each side yard opened, with no fences or other barrier. [My sister] Marjorie was often found in ours, holding forth to her dolls sitting meekly

Emil King took this picture in Fulda in about 1907. Some of the children must be his. He loved photographing his family.

in a row, while she labored as their teacher, using the side of the house for a blackboard and Mama's yardstick for a pointer. Our teachers would have been horrified to see us—any of us—playing teacher, for the play teacher spent most of her time in scolding and punishing her pupils. We didn't learn that from *our* teachers!

Polly Bullard, about 1900

In the corner of the front yard, near the sidewalk, was what I called my vine house. It was a thirty-six-inch wooden bench with spaced boards on three sides and the top, which someone had planted grapevines around. From spring until fall the structure was completely covered with leaves, except for the opening. Its entire floor space was no more than nine square feet and it was tall enough so that I could stand on the bench. To an adult it was probably only a seat. But to me, it was a complete world.

Evelyn Fairbanks, 1930s

In those times, you made your own games. One of our favorites was playing with paper dolls, and after the Depression you couldn't really afford having [store-bought] paper dolls, but we'd cut them out of the catalogs: the Sears Roebuck and Montgomery Ward catalogs, wherever there was the full person showing, and we would cut that out and that would be our paper dolls.

Marietta Neumann, 1930s

Of course, there was "pie," played with knives in the dirt, and hopscotch and jump rope, which we could not play on Sundays because we were wearing

Here's a tyke (we guess it's a boy with ringlets and patent-leather shoes) and good old wooden blocks in about 1900.

our good shoes. Jump rope started out as a nonthreatening game, but by the time we were ten years old and a second rope had been added, along with "hot peppers"—the turners turn the rope as fast as they can—we ended up with as many bruises from it as we did from roller skating.

Evelyn Fairbanks, 1930s

Everyone knew everyone else on the [St. Paul] city block where we lived. We played ball in the street. It was a real treat when the boys let any girl play. One time my brother George let me pitch. He batted left-handed so I wouldn't get hurt. He hit a line drive that struck me square in the belly and doubled me over. He was so proud of me when I didn't cry. (I couldn't!)

V. Lynette McKewin Kimble, 1930s

By the time I was eight, my favorite summer pastime was building. Scrounging orange crates for use as lumber was the most time-consuming part of the process. The best place to get them in our neighborhood was at the National Tea, the biggest grocery store of the three at the corner of 50th & Xerxes [in Minneapolis]. Summer after summer, [my brother] Steve and I,

Boys with big grins and skinny limbs duked it out in May 1947 at the Christ Child Center at 515 Partridge, St. Paul, a nonprofit neighborhood organization for immigrant families.

When athletic-equipment options were limited in 1944, these children performed their gymnastics on water pipes in Minneapolis.

or Gary Fadell, or Johnny Boettiger, took the wagon up to 50th and checked for boxes. Sometimes there was lots of them lying out in back if we were lucky enough to get there before they burned them. Sometimes there were so many crates we had to make a second trip. If there weren't any outside, we went in and asked the man working at the back of the store. When we decided to build a shack in the back yard, we returned to our faithful source of wood.

"Got any orange crates?" we asked hopefully in unison.

"Not today, boys," I heard as my heart sunk with disappointment, realizing that building plans would be delayed for lack of materials. "But I do have some peach boxes," he added, returning my hope once again.

Peach boxes only had a couple of good pieces of wood in them, but they were better than nothing. Orange crates were best. They had six long boards, two on each of three sides, separated by three thicker, square slabs of wood that were put together with little, zigzaggy metal things. It wasn't too often that we found crates that muskmelons came in, but they were different than the other boxes. The ends could be made into window frames without changing a thing, and the slats that made up the sides were perfect for making bars on windows, or for covering up places where things didn't quite fit.

Timothy Trent Blade, 1950

Thomas Dunning Rishworth helped a child with a new truck for Christmas in about 1955.

The Toy Industry Association and Forbes.com put together a list of some of the best-selling and best-loved toys of the last one hundred years:

1900s. Crayola crayons, introduced 1903. Also Lionel Trains (1900), Teddy bears (1903), Model T Ford die-cast car (1906).

1910s. Raggedy Ann dolls, 1915. Also Erector Sets (1913), Tinkertoys (1913), Lincoln Logs (1916).

A whole doll parade! This extravaganza took place in Winona in about 1930

Muriel Prindle on April 2, 1899 (isn't it fine when someone records the whole date and subject's name!), with her elaborate dollhouse

1920s. Madame Alexander collectible dolls, 1929. Madame Alexander was the first to create a doll based on a licensed character, Scarlett O'Hara from *Gone with the Wind.* Also the yo-yo (1929).

1930s. View-Master 3-D viewer, 1938. Also Sorry (1934), Monopoly (1935), Betsy Wetsy doll (1937).

1940s. Candy Land, 1949. Also Tonka Trucks, started near Lake Minnetonka in Mound (1947), Magic 8 Ball (1947), Scrabble (1948), Slinky (1948), Clue (1949).

1950s. Mr. Potato Head, 1952. Also Silly Putty (1952), LEGO building sets (1953), Matchbox Cars (1954), Play-Doh (1956), Yahtzee (1956), Frisbee (1957), Hula Hoop (1958), Barbie (1959).

1960s. G.I. Joe, 1964. Also Etch-a-Sketch (1960), Game of Life (1960), Troll Dolls (1961), Easy Bake Oven (1963), Operation (1965), Twister (1966), Battleship (1967), Lite Brite (1967), Hot Wheels (1968).

Forbes.com, December 2, 2005

Movies

Although it occurred nearly 70 years ago, I can still remember that some very unpleasant experiences were associated with the first movie that I attended. As a lad of about 10 years, I, in company with father and a brother, had viewed "The Great Train Robbery." The earlier movies had depicted several isolated, short acts with no special sequence, and "The Great Train Robbery" was said to have been the first narrative film—one that told a story. It was produced in 1903 and by 1905 it was a great hit in the so-called nickelodeons. These were movie theaters which charged a nickel for admission and were commonly known as the workingman's theater.

As might be expected, our village [Lanesboro] did not have a nickelodeon; so that first film was exhibited in a hall located over the corner drug store. While this was a silent film, I remember that the operator sought to heighten the theatrical effect by tapping on a table to simulate the sound of the horses' hoofs as the robbers rode along. Even without the accompanying sounds of the fighting and shooting of a modern movie, I was sufficiently impressed and disturbed so as to cause me to have some terrifying nightmares for more than one night thereafter.

Gerhard A. Ellestad

When my brother, George, was ten, and I was eight, in 1932, we were given an allowance of fifteen cents each and every Saturday. Before the afternoon was over, we had spent it all. The movies were ten cents, and we could buy three quarter-pound candy bars for a dime. Usually George chose a Baby Ruth, and I a Snickers, and we split a Mounds Bar. Mounds came in two pieces so we didn't have to argue over which of us got the bigger half.

The movies were at the St. Clair, the Uptown or the Grandview. We walked to the theater, and we walked home [1371 Fairmount Avenue, St. Paul]. As the movies started at 2, we would leave home before 1:15, and when we arrived at the theater we stood in line waiting for the doors to open.

Our parents helped us select the movie choice for the week as we looked in the paper. My brother and I always went together, sometimes taking a friend apiece along with us, but few of our friends were so fortunate as to have such a large allowance. [His family wasn't hit so severely by the

At Duluth's ornate Zelda Theater, lads looked over the offering—Cecil B. DeMille's 1919 film drama, *For Better, For Worse.* The theater boasted a Pipe Organ DeLuxe.

Depression as many others; his father kept his job as a sales manager.] Our sister never went with us.

Once I lost my dime on the way to the St. Clair Theater and stood in front of the place crying my eyes out. Of course, we had the two extra nickels, but that would mean we couldn't buy our candy.

The manager of the theater came to my rescue. He knelt in front of me and asked piercing questions about whether I had truly lost the money. Apparently he was satisfied, and I was allowed to enter the darkened theater with my brother. I don't remember if we ever found the lost dime, but I know we each had our fill of candy before returning home.

Robert Williams McKewin

Celebrations

FACING PAGE
Mary Warneke held
the cake, with children
gathered around her
in Anoka County in
about 1905.

Life is sweetest when the ones we love are smiling. Some of our most vivid memories are centered on parties, holidays, and food. We still can almost smell the turkey in the oven, the Malt-O-Meal on the stove, and the candles woofed out on the birthday cake.

Birthdays

The first birthday present of my memory was a hat. As I came downstairs I heard Pa say to Ma, "Shall we give her the present before breakfast?" I said, "Oh, I won't eat it!" It didn't occur to me that it could be anything but a stick of candy or some such little thing.

Pa deliberated, "Well, perhaps if she is sure she won't eat it." After I had convinced them of this, they brought out a new hat, the first one I ever had. It was a black velvet with a magenta ribbon hanging down the back. I thought it beautiful. It lasted several years, of course, for a Sunday hat.

Anna Lathrop Clary, 1860s

Rochester Minnesota
July 20, 1876

Dear Grandma [in Vermont],

As I have not written to you in a long while, I now take the privilege of doing so. As I am interested in most every body's birthday, I like to know what they get. Please tell me what you got . . .

Perhaps you don't know what I got for my birthday so I will tell you. a book couple of aprons two pair of hose kid gloves ribbon crocheted sacque a couple of pictures a bed-spread a washdish some lace curtains a commode for my room . . . I want you to write me a great long letter as soon as you can. I must close.

Your Grandchild

Althea Stebbins

We know this child's birthday party in about 1940 was at the posh residence of Mrs. S. Awes. That's probably Mrs. Sigbert Awes at 4253 Lyndale Avenue South in Minneapolis. Let's assume those aren't all her kids.

FORMER GOVERNOR ALEXANDER RAMSEY'S JOURNAL, OCTOBER 21, 1887: BIRTHDAY PARTY [FOR HIS GRANDSON RAMSEY'S TENTH BIRTHDAY], ABOUT A HALF DOZEN WERE PRESENT HERE AND MADE THE EVENING HIDEOUS.

Wed. June 28 1911

To-day is my [eleventh] BIRTHDAY. Got up irly this morn. Had berecfast and at my plate thar wer the pakagis.

No. 1. Water Babys [probably the children's fairy-tale novel popular in that time].

No. 2. Kiplings boy storys.

No. 3. A grate big stick of candy. And sonething I did not see at first. 2 lovely necties.

Glanville Smith

My birthday party, July 16, 1911. I am 12 years old. 7 girls came and surprised me. I had fell down so I was going up stairs in the bathroom and put something on [it] and they all yelled out surprise. There was Beatrice Johnson, Helen Arnston, Evelyn Arntson, Mildred Haben, Selma Jellum, Ruth Mavall, Viva Jost. We all came down stairs and I unwrapped my presents. There was a book, hairpin box, 1 cup and saucer, a box of writing paper, a postal card, and a bracelet from Mother. We went on the side porch and played games. It

In about 1955, when children still got all dressed up for birthday parties, Paula Thompson celebrated with her friends in St. Paul.

Three's company: "Happy birthday triplets," the cake says. Second birthday, would you guess?

Oh, how sweet! Just how many years does the one candle represent?

got so cold that we had to come in the house. Then we went and played the piano and sang songs. Then mother called us for refreshments. We went and ate. We had ice cream, cake, nabisgoes [Nabisco wafers], candy, and water . . . We played the phonograph.

Ruth Marion Skoglund

The Children's Party Book *by Marion Jane Parker in 1924 had suggestions for games at birthday parties. Here's "You Auto Know":*

> A great many children take pride in their ability to recognize the make of an automobile at a glance. Try these questions on them and find out how familiar they are with the names.
>
> What auto is called after a former President? (Lincoln)
> What do you do when in the path of an auto? (Dodge)
> What auto will find a person in a hotel? (Paige)
> What auto is seen in the sky? (Moon)
> What auto has the same name as a famous battle in American history? (Lexington)
> What auto has the same name as a famous river? (Hudson)
> What auto is named after a famous Revolutionary General? (Lafayette)

Friday March 3 [1933]

Today was my birthday. Got a boy scout shirt from Grandma. Got a swell suit from Daddy: a lot of streetcar tokens & 50 cents from Mother; one dollar from the girls. Hopped a truck to Sanitary Food. Got a jigsaw puzzle & went to Hamline [Theater] and saw Wallace Benny in "Flesh."

William M. Cummings didn't know until he was an adult that his parents had told him a fib about his birth date. He was not born March 3, 1918. He actually was born three and a half months earlier—November 18, 1917. His sister told him the truth when he was in his thirties. His mother had been pregnant with him when she married his father. In those days, "having to get married" was a grave social embarrassment.

"Just get 'em out of the house!" This birthday party was at an ice cream parlor in 1973, when most kids still celebrated birthdays at home.

Holidays

Ruth Marion Skoglund kept a tiny diary when she was eleven to thirteen years old and living in Red Wing. A girl of few words, she wrote short entries in tiny penmanship. She made no mention of how she felt about clothes or her looks or helping her mother around the house. Only rarely did she tell about her emotions other than she "had fun." But holidays! She rarely missed noting them:

2–14–1911: I got 34 Valentines & one box of bonbons from brother Walter, a heart shape.

4–1–1911. I got fooled about 3 times.

5–30–1911. Memorial Day. Have no school, went up to the semitary with Mother and Mildred.

9–7. Went to the State Fair.

7–2–1912. Went downtown and bought some firecrackers.

Dec. 24, 1911. Have a Christmas tree.

July 7, 1861

On the 4th of July I went to the Methodist picnic [probably in St. Paul]. There girls vs. the boys through firecrackers at each other after refreshments, during which many holes were burnt in each other's clothing. I got behind a tree near a party of 5 girls, who were doing the most damage to the boys, so that they not see me. I kept tossing into them all, busting under and over them. I burnt about a dozen holes in the dress of one of them. After a while the girls stopped partly for the want of fire-crackers and torpedoes and partly on account of holes & burns. One boy had a blister on the back of his neck, and I had four small holes [in my clothes]. Just before refreshments, the Declaration of Independence was read. In the evening we fired off 3 sky-rockets, 6 serpants, 5 pinwheels, 1 grasshopper. During the day, 12 packs fire-crackers, 6 packs torpedoes.

Frederick Allis

Sometimes we went to town and saw the [Fourth of July] parade. There would be bands, and the Civil War veterans would be there in their blue uniforms, all marching. Our neighbors would come in too in the buckboards, bringing picnic lunches to eat. They would always fill the buckboards with hay so the children could lie down and sleep. The Fourth always gave us a good chance to see our neighbors. I remember one neighbor wagon going by. They had cut down little trees and stuck them in the sides of the wagon so they could have shade.

Lillian MacGregor Shaw, early 1900s

Jewell Peterson, her hair in amazing corkscrews, showed her patriotic pride in about 1908. Her father was Swedish immigrant Axel L. Peterson, owner of a general store in Hawley. Axel was a tremendous promoter, staging campaigns such as coffee-drinking contests. He was not above getting his kids into the act. Jewell's costume might have been part of an ad scheme.

If you ever lived in North Minneapolis, Pumpkin Joe Greenstein would need no introduction. He gained his moniker, the "Pumpkin Man," from his pumpkin distribution of the 1930s to 1960s to North Minneapolis school children. He claimed, as a boy, he never could afford a pumpkin so he stole one. Thus, the children of North Minneapolis would always be provided with pumpkins.

A typical Pumpkin Day would begin early with farmers from Anoka, Champlin and other now-northern suburbs of Minneapolis dropping off their pumpkins for the distribution. The bushels would take up most of the east lane of Plymouth Avenue. For the rest of the day, traffic would be diverted.

Novelties like livestock would then need to be put in place. Besides floats, carriages and animal pens, some of the more creative novelties included a goat bathtub where goats would be bathed in confetti, and a life-size replica of the "Sputnik" satellite (supposedly landing in North Minneapolis from Russia).

The press from television and newspapers would be on hand as the distribution began. Dozens of Jefferson and Greyhound Lines buses would donate their services transporting children to and from the grocery store. Children would go through the rows of pumpkins, looking for a choice Jack O'Lantern. Always in attendance was a television personality children could recognize. Usually a politician or two would also make an appearance.

Loads of pumpkins were sent directly to various schools not making the trip to the store. In all, in any given year, several thousands of pumpkins were given out by the Pumpkin Man.

In 1946, children
gathered for a Halloween
party at 271 Maria
Avenue, St. Paul.

My father [Pumpkin Joe] told me the only years there were no Pumpkin Days were during World War II. A sign was placed on the grocery-store door stating, "Store closed. Off to fight the war."

Larry Greenstein

Nov. 28, 1862

Today is Thanksgiving day according to the Proclamation of Gov. Ramsey . . . Ma invited Mr. Davel and wife to dine with us, but they were not well. Ma then invited Mr. Prescott and wife, but they had promised to go somewhere else. Ma then invited the Chamblins, but their children were sick, so nobody ate with us. We had oyster soup, chicken pie, potato, plum pudding, mince pie, apple pie, whortleberry pie, raisins, almonds, pecan nuts. We were going to have a lot more if anybody came.

Frederick Allis

Thursday, Nov. 29, 1866. Thanksgiving Day. Staid at home. Eat and Stuffed myself with Turkey.

Frank Folsom

In those early frontier days it was not common to have Christmas trees in the homes. I never heard of one except in stories of rich people in the cities. But we did have Christmas trees at Sunday School. My first was a terrible disappointment at its beginning. For all I could see in the little church was a calico curtain. After what seemed like a very long time, we heard Christmas carols; the curtain was drawn aside and there stood a beautiful, beautiful Christmas tree, trimmed with lights [burning candles] and long strings of popcorn and cranberries.

John Spaniol, front, and his cousin Greg Neyssen were mighty impressed with the Thanksgiving turkey in about 1950.

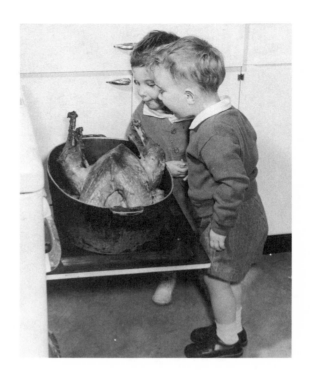

In 1899, Muriel Prindle displayed her dolls in the family home at 1605 East Second Street, Duluth. Her father, William M. Prindle, was a realtor in Duluth for fifty-seven years and prominent in mining development. The home certainly shows his wealth, doesn't it?

On that tree each family had its family presents. The result was that some children received only the Sunday School bag of candy and had the doubtful pleasure of seeing their more fortunate friends receive real presents. But I felt rich, because some lady gave me a beautiful doll about six inches long, with yellow china hair, elegantly dressed in green silk; and the Sunday School superintendent, who kept a hardware store, gave me a little red toy dustpan.

Anna Lathrop Clary, 1860s

I remember the Christmas of that year [1861] more vividly than any other of my childhood. Minnie and I each had a pink calico apron, a stick of striped candy, an apple and a doll about seven inches long, with china head, hands and feet. That was the first apple I ever saw, and the doll was the first and only I ever had.

Alice Mendenhall George

Did somebody get a little boy as a Christmas gift? No: that was Edward F. Fairbrother with the loot under the tree on Christmas Day 1901. Note the spectacular popcorn garlands. The Fairbrother family lived at 687½ Central Avenue in St. Paul. Apparently the family hung presents in the tree after opening. Good news: we don't have to listen to Edward learning the drum.

Walter Stone Pardee in 1866 was a fourteen-year-old homesick boy recently arrived from New England. More than fifty years later, he recalled a Christmas party that year given in Minneapolis by Mr. and Mrs. John T. Blaisdell. It featured a sleigh ride on a farm that later became Blaisdell's Addition to the city of Minneapolis.

Likely there were 20 children on hand. Long before dark Mr. Blaisdell got all who cared to go into his big farm sleigh that was bedded in straw, and he took us for a ride to the back of his farm, half a mile west, and this was at Lyndale Avenue of today [written in the early 1920s]. The air was crisp, clear and cold, and boys and girls especially were wonderfully stimulated to enjoy the substantial food soon to be offered. The road was out of the common way . . . Not a house was to be seen along the route, very likely, in the region where there are hundreds of costly homes [today] . . . But that 1866 afternoon, our brisk team pulled us merrily along thru snow drifts on a just plain farm upon much of which Mr. Blaisdell raised wheat. As to houses in sight over on Nicollet Avenue, there were only two or three such as would be on 160-acre farms. A little white schoolhouse some way out was the biggest building to be seen, until far away at Lake Street were two or three farmhouses.

Our ride was cold, the sun set early and soon we were back to a most hospitable home, permeated with good cheer . . . The table was piled with the substantial and the fine . . . What wonders there were in the way of broiled chicken, for instance, the hearty vegetables, the appetizing jellies and the cakes, pies and puddings so dear to the heart and so satisfying to the stomach of the small boy.

And now came the jolly evening. The host looked after the interests of all; Mrs. Blaisdell was kindness and tact in essence.

*   *   *

Oh! Such a Christmas. It was typical of the Swedish ones. The first course was lutefisk with a white-sauce gravy which had just a little dry mustard added to it. The next was yard-length sausages and cranberry sauce, which contained the whole berry, and many other trimmings, and the last was rice steamed in whole milk. This . . . [mother] always emptied into a little stone crock, and on top for decoration she put on a few raisins because there wasn't enough to appease even a child's appetite. Even so we never had thought for complaints. For good behavior (maybe) we got a white sugar cookie which contained caraway seed. All this made a wonderful Christmas dinner. We never exchanged presents but we exchanged hospitality with our friends.

Annie Swanson Gaslin, about 1880

Marjorie Bullard kept a diary of her school life and social activities as a teenager in St. Paul. Here's what she recorded about her family on Christmas Day, 1897.

Early this morning, Betty called out to me, "Merry Christmas." I suppose she thought she had waked me up but she was mistaken. We dressed very quickly and I went down to Polly's and Betty's room. They had to get several things

Ralph, Dorothy, and William Gardner were home at 369 Jay Street (now Galtier), St. Paul, for Christmas 1912, with a fine collection of gifts.

Muriel Prindle, left, with an unnamed cousin as elves, in 1899. Notice the l-o-n-g stockings, hung with care.

out of Emma's room that were too large to take down the night before. At last when all was ready we went down. What should we see but three chairs which looked like those of Papa, Mamma and Baby Bear's. There was one which we all gave to Papa, one that Uncle gave to Papa and Mamma, and one from Mamma to me. It is a lovely red chair and just right for me, and Papa likes it better than his own. Under my stocking was a big book filled with 19 of Mozart's sonatas, from Papa; "The Last Days of Pompeii," from Polly, and a picture with a large frame from Kate. Also there was some blue flannel for a dressing-jacket from Mamma. And in my stocking was a little glove-buttoner [a tool to work tiny buttons on long gloves] from Betty. Mamma thought the irons which I gave her were fine, and she says she shall want to use them right away. The bag that Polly and I gave Betty she likes very much and goes around carrying it on her arm all the time.

When we were having breakfast, Amelia and Theodore came over too to bring me a little knife. They had to carry a lot of things around to people living on the "hill." When we had washed the dishes, we admired our presents and ate candy. About 12 o'clock Betty and I walked up to Grandma's . . . Dinner was ready.

We had the tree right after dinner and it was lovely. We all had lovely presents, and especially Grandma. Her lap was full and she kept saying, "I have so many more presents than the rest of you." Not very long after we went home, and it seemed as it always does—very lonesome—to get home with the house all dark.

It has been altogether a very happy Christmas Day.

*   *   *

I can't remember when I ever believed in Santa Claus. It just didn't sound true, that anybody could go up on the housetops with reindeer and all that stuff. But I went along with it. It was a very good story to tell. One night—I'm not sure which Christmas—my sister Laura got up in the night to see if anybody had a doll in their stocking. She found that she did have one, but that Mae had a nicer one. So she switched them. But mother knew the difference. She switched them back. Mother really laid down the law.

Lillian MacGregor Shaw, early 1900s

The Sky Room, atop Dayton's downtown Minneapolis store, was the scene of a children's breakfast with Santa on December 13, 1961.

The western look, hot in 1951: Mike and Harry Sieben in their new Hopalong Cassidy outfits. Hopalong was the star of the first network television series, beginning in 1949, and he was featured on everything from wristwatches to lunch boxes to children's dishes. The Sieben boys also went on to fame—in the Minnesota legislature.

In this posed photo, a smiling woman taught a child how to winnow wild rice in about 1938. Note the drums in the background.

Food

Charles Eastman as a boy asked his uncle why the Great Mystery gave such power and food to the white man. He recorded his uncle's response this way:

The greatest object of their lives seems to be to acquire possessions—to be rich. They desire to possess the whole world. For thirty years they were trying to entice us to sell them our land. Finally the outbreak [the Dakota War of 1862] gave them all, and we have been driven away from our beautiful country.

They are a wonderful people. They have divided the day into hours, like the moons of the year. In fact, they measure everything. Not one of them would let so much as a turnip go from his field unless he received full value for it. I understand that their great men make a feast and invite many, but when the feast is over the guests are required to pay for what they have eaten before leaving the house. I myself saw at White Cliff (the name given to St. Paul, Minnesota) a man who kept a brass drum and a bell to call people to his table; but when he got them in he would make them pay for the food!

Charles Eastman, 1860s

Dec. 19, 1862

After breakfast I went to the butcher's and got: 2 prairie chickens, 8 porter house steaks, 1 porter house roast, 1 soup bone, 2 dozen eggs. Then I went home. As soon as I got home ma sent me down again with a pail, I got 6 qt of cranberries at Chamblin's. I went over to Comb's and told him I wanted 6 oz. each of Essence of Almond and of Pineapple, but Mr. Combs said he had none. So I went up to Day and Jenk's and got a bottle of Essence of Almond containing 2 oz. Then I went home . . . I then went to Temple and Beaupres and got 6 lb. of almonds. I cracked the 6 lb. of almonds and ate 1 to every handful I cracked.

Frederick Allis

[After moving to Minneapolis from New York City,] We soon became acquainted with a man with a horse and wagon. He was Aunt Fanny's father. He used to come up the street . . . shouting "Vatermelone! Big Vatermelone!" When he got to our house, Mr. Hymes would get down from the perch and go up to the house and ring the bell. Mama would greet him with, "Machitan, was teest due?" "In-law, how are you?" Then they both proceeded to the wagon to inspect the produce. Mama always had him take a core out of the watermelon that he was pushing to sell. Depending on finances, she'd buy a whole, a half or a quarter. When it came to oranges, she never bought a whole dozen, only a half dozen. She would cut them in half, and each of us would get a piece of orange. With apples, she dickered for a half-bushel. They would be put in the cellar for later use.

Mama and the fruit peddler always dickered for items yet to be on the market. Early in the season, she'd put in orders for cabbage for sauerkraut, red tomatoes for canning, green tomatoes for pickling, cucumbers for pickling, and peaches and blue plums for sauces and jellies. Our cellar was full of good stuff for winter. We loved the peppers and pimentos too. Mama learned most of this canning stuff from the settlement house, the Southside Neighborhood House. In New York, no one canned because of space limitations. In the old country, the food stuff wasn't available, but in America it was good!

Fannie S. Schanfield, 1920s

Our cellar was an exciting place from October on. There was a large bin of potatoes, and cabbages hung from the beams by their roots or stalks. A ham or two also hung from the beams, and beets, carrots, parsnips and turnips were all buried in the sand on the floor. Pumpkins and Hubbard squash were stored on a big hanging shelf, and there was a 100-pound bag of onions, and countless jars and glasses and crocks of jams, jellies, preserves, apple butter, pickles—and at least a hundred jars of tomatoes, the only vegetable Mother ever canned.

There was also a side of bacon hanging from the beams, and a kit of mackerel (that is, mackerel in a wooden pail) and a long, narrow box of herring, the little ones about six inches long and brown. And Aunt Fanny and Uncle Arthur used to bring us a firkin of butter and a side of salt pork

Corn on the cob must be little Grace Linde's favorite food in about 1913.

several times during the winter. Sometimes, too, there would even be a little keg of green grapes in sawdust, but otherwise we had no vegetables or fruits out of season. We lived on the root vegetables that could be stored in the cellar, and during the winter months bought only fresh meat, milk and cream. Our flour and sugar were bought and stored in quantity, and all baked goods were made at home.

Even our coffee was bought in bulk, 25 pounds of the green beans at one time. Sunday morning, while the rest of the family attended church, Grandpa would put a pound or so in a long iron dripping-pan in the oven, turning the beans over and over with a long iron spoon until they were just the right rich brown. He did enough at one time for a week's supply, and it was ground fresh each morning. Mother put it on the stove in an iron pot, in cold water, with a dash of salt and an eggshell, as well as the white of the egg, brought it to a boil and immediately set it back on the reservoir to keep hot. The coffee aroma that filled the house each morning was something today's coffee makers [in the late 1950s] will never produce!

Blanche Stoddard Seely, 1880s

Before Christmas, mother would be planning for weeks for what we'd have for dinner. It was always a turkey or a goose which we had raised ourselves. Usually it was a goose for New Year's and a turkey for Christmas Eve. We'd

Hungry fellows scarfed down supper at the Square Lake Boy Scout Camp in about 1945. The two-fisted approach was most effective.

always start cutting from the bottom, lift the upper layers off and eat from the bottom up. The Christmas cake we usually finished on New Year's Eve. The goose always served a double purpose because every drop of fat was saved for goose grease, a standby medicine used the whole year. It was rubbed on externally, taken internally for colds—or anything else for that matter—from aching joints to congested lungs.

When I was a kid, I had a terribly big appetite. I could digest anything. One night I had a cold and was coughing. Mother put a great big cup of goose grease on the table by the side of my bed. She told me that if I got coughing in the night to take a big spoonful of goose grease. Sure enough, I got coughing. So I took a spoonful. Gee, it tasted good. Like New Year's dinner. So I took some more, and by and by I had drunk it all down. Next morning when I confessed, mother said, "I meant to take only one spoonful." But I got no indigestion. Went right to sleep.

Lillian MacGregor Shaw, about 1900

We often had gingerbread when we came home from school. It was so good that a friend of mine, Rose Demel, once asked me to trade an egg for a piece of mother's gingerbread. Mother's kolaches also were very good. She set up her dough in the attic on Friday nights because it was warm up there. On Saturday mornings she would take the dough down and make about four pans of wonderful kolaches with prune, poppy seed, and fruit fillings. It was usually my job to pit the prunes. The kolaches were always gone after Sunday breakfast.

Emily Panushka Erickson, 1910s

Two toddlers enjoyed their favorite treat at a Minneapolis maternity hospital in 1925.

The Farmer, *published in St. Paul, called itself "the northwest's only weekly farm paper." Each month from February 1929 to January 1931, it ran "Betty's Scrapbook of Little Recipes for Little Cooks." The publication said Betty was a real girl, seven years old when the series began, who carefully tried each recipe to find the right ingredients and methods. Her mother, Mrs. R. C. Dahlberg, helped. (Quite a bit, apparently.)* The Farmer *didn't say where they lived. Betty ran recipes for such treats as cocoa, popovers, and scrambled eggs. Here's her potato advice:*

Let's try some baked potatoes

Dear Little Cooks: When I want to bake potatoes, I first see that there is a good hot fire, for the oven [woodstove] must be hot. Then I go down cellar and pick out as many nice, smooth, sound-looking potatoes as I think we can eat. I try to get them all about the same size and a little larger than the average.

When I have them up in the kitchen, I put them into a pan of water and scrub them very clean.

My potatoes are ready for the oven now, and I put them in on the grate to bake. It takes from forty-five to sixty minutes for baking, depending on the size of the potatoes and the heat of the oven.

Some people like to grease the skin of the potatoes well before they put them in to bake; it makes the skins softer. Now look after the fire again so the oven will keep hot.

The kids' table in about 1946, with forties wallpaper in the background. Do you remember the honor of graduating to the adult table?

When it is time for the potatoes to be done, I take a clean holder in my right hand and open the oven door with my left hand. I reach in and pick up a potato and squeeze it gently in the holder. If it seems all soft, it is done; if not, it needs more baking.

Although plain baked potatoes are very good, eaten piping hot with good gravy or plenty of butter, you may like to try a little different way of fixing them, one which mother may not have time for very often. [Betty then explained how to make stuffed baked potatoes.]

*   *   *

The food [for Sunday picnics] was brought out of the bottom of the basket with the seriousness of a sacrifice. And for good reason. It was almost always perfectly prepared. Spotless laundry and superb cooking were two skills expected among the church women. I remember how ruthlessly Florence Wilson was teased, for several Sundays, because her candied yams were too dry.

Besides candied yams there were greens, alone or mixed—collard, turnip, mustard, and dandelion—cooked with salt pork, bacon ends, or ham, which produced the pot likker that Daddy was so crazy about. There were navy, northern, or green beans, or black-eyed peas, also cooked with salt pork, bacon ends, or ham.

There was always chicken. It was fried or smothered in gravy or baked. If the chicken was baked, there was cornbread dressing. And there was ham and sometimes beef or pork roast. In season there was rabbit, squirrel, and fish. For dessert there were layered cakes with homemade jelly filling; fruit pies with crust that really did melt in your mouth; lemon meringue pies

Can you guess the date of this kitchen photograph? We believe it was about 1950. That's likely mom and son on the right and an extension agent on the left, making a visit to teach homemaking skills.

with peaks, valleys, and caves displaying a rainbow of browns; sweet potato pies, each made from a different recipe; and my favorite—peach cobbler. And there were jars and jars of homemade relishes made from cucumbers, tomatoes, onions, green and red peppers, beets, and watermelon rind.

The children sat at tables separate from the grown-ups. But there were at least two pairs of eyes on us at all times.

Evelyn Fairbanks, 1930s

Back then, north Minneapolis was largely a community of Jewish cooks. Every household had one. The foods and meals were basically the same, but each household prepared them a little differently, depending upon which part of the old world their grandparents or parents immigrated from. Every home had a different smell, but it was still the smell of borscht, kugel and flanken [pot roast]. I remember walking by people's open windows during warm weather and smelling all their cooking. In winter, when the windows were closed, they were covered with steam from the cooking.

We were kept warm by chicken soup on Fridays and barley soup during the rest of the week. We had stews cooked with fresh potatoes, delicious kosher meat, and tons of carrots, celery, and onions. It would all cook slowly, and the wonderful, mouth-watering smell of natural juice would fill our kitchen and waft into our bedrooms while we were doing our homework. Our kitchen always felt warm, even though our bedrooms were freezing. (In those days, it was thought to be healthier if you slept in the cold.)

One memory I'll never forget is breakfast on winter mornings. My mom would cook hot cereal, usually Cream of Wheat or Malt-O-Meal, and toast to fill our stomachs and warm us up before school. I would love the smell of the cereal cooking on the stove—a warm, smooth, soft smell that invited us into the kitchen. I almost didn't mind waking on cold mornings because I'd be welcomed by the smell. It would be pitch black outside, but then I'd go into the kitchen with all the lights on and all the breakfast smells, and my dad would be sitting at the table listening to the news on WCCO and eating. (Growing up, I almost never saw my parents go to sleep or wake up. I only saw them in other rooms in our house, always awake and always fully dressed.)

Sandra Kreamer, 1940s–50s

Sitting on the curb of Winona's East Third Street, three children got their fill of hotcakes during the 1938 Pancake Days.

Posing for a Minneapolis newspaper photographer in 1955, these cooks had a plate of pastries ready for tasting. They must have cleaned up the kitchen before the visitor came.

Historic Events

Wars and the Great Depression have taken their toll on Minnesota's children, from a fifteen-year-old slogging through the South as a Civil War drummer boy to a girl terrified that World War II enemies were under her bed.

Civil and Dakota Wars

William Bircher was fifteen years old when the Civil War began. Yearning for adventure, the boy from West St. Paul Township ran away from home to join the Union Army. He was rejected because he was too young. But William had another plan. He went home and persuaded his father to join up, too. The army took them both. They were assigned to the Second Minnesota Volunteer Regiment, Company K, in August 1861. William became a drummer boy; his father, a farmer, handled animals pulling wagons. At first, William was overjoyed. He kept a diary, added thoughts later and published it as a book in 1889.

> The happiest day of my life, I think, was when I donned my blue uniform and received my new drum. Now, at last, after so many efforts, I was really a full-fledged drummer and going South to do and die for my county if need be.

But by January, the thrill was gone.

> We commenced our march [through Kentucky] in a terrific rain and thunderstorm. The water came down in torrents, and streams of mud and water ran along the turnpike, through which we were compelled to wade and plod our way. We saw that a soldier's life was not so fine as we as schoolboys had seen it pictured in our histories.

It was worse in April, when William saw the aftermath of the Battle of Shiloh in Tennessee. The Confederate forces had launched a surprise attack against the Union Army, but General Grant's men prevailed.

> What a horrible sight met our gaze. Dead men [probably both Union and Confederate] were lying in the mud, mixed up with sacks of grain and government stores, some lying in the water and others trampled entirely

out of sight in the deep mud. This was where the great stampede occurred. No pen can picture the horrors of this part of the field . . .

The battlefield was strewn with the wreck and carnage of war. Caissons, dismounted cannon, and dead artillery horses and their dead riders were piled up in heaps, and the warm sun caused a stench that was almost unbearable. Here and there we could see where a wounded soldier had been pinned to the ground by a fallen limb of a tree. The shells setting fire to the dry leaves, the poor fellows had been burned alive to a crisp. No historian can ever depict the horrors of a battlefield. The dead lying in every direction and in every stage of decomposition. Squads of men scattered all over the field digging trenches, rolling the dead in, and covering them up with three or four inches of dirt, only to be washed off by the first rain, leaving the bones to be picked by the buzzards and crows. Such is the terror of war.

William kept track of the miles he marched from 1861 to 1865—more than five thousand. He often was very cold; one time in Kentucky, he and his comrades stood by a fire all night to keep from freezing. He had no shoes at one point and wrapped his bare feet with the pocket he tore from his shirt. Food rations usually were short. Thirsty, he once dipped a spoon in a puddle and strained the water through his dirty, sweaty handkerchief. His unit was shot at and engaged in hand-to-hand combat. His body was covered with vermin. Even Christmas was dark, cold, and dreary in camp.

Yet, amazingly, William Bircher and his father got home safely—never wounded, never very sick. In May of 1865 he marched back to Fort Snelling and headed home. Later, William ran a popular saloon known as Billy Bircher's Place in West St. Paul, married, and had three children. He was always known for his sense of humor, as evident in the diary record he made after the bloody Battle of Chickamauga in Georgia. His unit helped the nurses.

During my stay in the hospital, which was filled with sick and wounded, some ladies from the North visited them daily, bringing with them delicacies of every kind, and did all they could to cheer and comfort the suffering. On one occasion, a pretty miss of sixteen, who came down with her mother, was distributing reading material and speaking gentle words of encouragement to those around. She overheard a soldier exclaim, "Oh, my Lord!" Stepping up to his bedside to rebuke him for profanity, she remarked, "Didn't I hear you call upon the name of the Lord? I am one of His daughters. Is there anything I can do for you?"

Looking up in her bright face, he replied, "I don't know but what there is." Raising his eyes to hers, and extending his hand, he said, "Please ask Him to make me His son-in-law."

*   *   *

Soon there came marching back the remnants of the gallant regiments of Minnesota that had shown their mettle on many battlefields and at the Little Round Top at Gettysburg. They were to be mustered out at Fort Snelling. I have heard my parents tell of the mingled joy, suspense, and heartbreak of these scenes, but only the excitement of marching columns affected us as children.

One more event from the past in our life at the fort flashes out with startling clearness—the visit to the Northwest of General U. S. Grant. On the great day within the fort along the officers' row all the families were gathered, the children as near the drive as possible. At last, sitting on the back seat of an open landau [a horse-drawn, four-wheeled enclosed carriage] was the general! We knew him from his pictures; stocky, in the familiar broad-brimmed hat with its gold cord and tassel, the crimson sash, and the gold epaulet on his blue coat. The carriage stopped at the commandant's door and the famous guest was escorted through the spacious hall to the great bastion at the rear, where the ladies of the fort had prepared for his coming. The children, of course, were not present at the reception, but afterwards, believe it or not, I drank out of the same barrel of lemonade that General Grant was served from.

Mary Newson

During the Civil War, when her father, Alexander Ramsey, was a U.S. senator in Washington, Marion Ramsey was enrolled in a Philadelphia boarding school. She had time for an adventure when she was about eleven:

Before I left Washington I did one thing, and quite of my own volition, too, which has been a source of infinite satisfaction to me all my life. Without the knowledge of anyone in the family, I and a small friend a year or two older dressed ourselves in our best clothes and walked up Pennsylvania Avenue to the White House. It was a reception day when anyone, high or low, black or white, might call on the president. We followed the crowd and presently entered the room where Mr. Lincoln stood. The marshal of the district beside him introduced us, having first learned our names. Mr. Lincoln, with his tall figure, had to lean over as he shook hands with us and repeated our names, with just as much "empressement" [animated eagerness] as for any of the callers. I can still see the large hand encased in a white glove, all the fingers extended, and the rugged face as it bent over us. I never saw Mr. Lincoln again, though I watched the crowds as they passed along Chestnut Street in Philadelphia on their [way] to Independence Hall, where his body lay in state in April of 1865.

Marion Ramsey Furness, 1864

A woman and child were imprisoned at Fort Snelling after the Dakota War.

PUBLISHED BY WHITNEY'S GALLERY, ST. PAUL, MINN.

Mahpiyago-wig (Blue Sky Woman) was born in 1848 at the Khemnichan or Red Wing village, near what's now the Red Wing depot. In only a few years, the Dakota people were forced to relinquish their land in accordance with the Treaty of 1851. The government expected the Mdewakanton and other Dakota bands to move to reservation lands on the Minnesota River.

When she was fourteen, she went to Birch Coulee, near present-day Morton, to help relatives, intending to return home in August. But the Dakota War broke out around her. The military captured her and her mother, Wamndiwig (Eagle Woman). They and sixteen hundred Dakota were imprisoned at Fort Snelling through the winter of 1863. The knowledge of where plants would live under cover of snow helped them survive.

The following summer, a steamboat carried Mahpiyago-wig and the other Dakota down the Mississippi River and back up the Missouri River to Fort Thompson on Crow Creek in South Dakota. On the trip, many who had survived the prison camp died, including her mother. Crow Creek was a brutal, barren region, very different from their abundant homelands. Little food, water, or shelter existed. Nothing would grow. No materials were available for clothing. Children died, many from starvation. Eventually, Mahpiyago-wig and other survivors were transferred to the Santee Reservation in Nebraska.

In 1879, Mahpiyago-Wig, by then called Julia Frazier, married Hdakin-kinyanna (Walking Softly at Dawn), also called Thomas Rouillard. They made their way back to Minnesota, and by 1887 the family was in Prairie Island. She gave birth to ten children, but only two survived to adulthood.

Goodhue County Historical Society

* * *

Mary Newson's father, Thomas McLean Newson, was a deputy at Fort Snelling during the war. His family lived there with him, and Mary got an eyeful and earful.

In our play about the parade ground [at Fort Snelling, where her family lived], we often watched with frightened delight the two captive Indians, leaders in the Sioux War, each dragging a cannon ball chained to his left leg, while under guard he swept the walks. Medicine Bottle was a coarse, brutal creature who often showed to visitors his arm tattooed with the symbols indicating the men, women, and children he had scalped, about fifty in all. Shakopee, or Little Six, was interesting and intelligent. When after many delays and reprieves the orders for their execution came from Washington, the two were finally hung. The gallows was erected outside the fort on a little knoll, commanding a view of the hills across the Minnesota River and Pilot Knob . . . All the children of the garrison, save only ourselves, were allowed to be present at the hanging. However, I recall most distinctly that from some vantage point I saw in the distance the crowds, the scaffold, and the swinging bodies. I listened with eagerness as my father recounted to my mother a dramatic incident connected with the event. As the black cap was about to be drawn over the head of Shakopee, a railway whistle woke the echoes along the bluffs and the first train of cars pulled into Mendota. With a tragic gesture of dignity, the chief raised his arm and pointing across the river said, "As the white man comes in, the Indian goes out." The next moment the trap fell.

World War I

A boy bade his uncle good-bye in St. Paul in 1917, World War I time. The soldier probably was headed to Camp Dodge, near Des Moines, Iowa. Everybody wore hats in those days.

During the Great War, tensions ran high in a state settled by Europeans. These children held anti-German signs in 1917 or 1918.

Kids helped with a scrap paper drive on downtown Duluth's West First Street in 1918, under the auspices of the Red Cross. Many kinds of salvage were collected for the war drive. The building at the far right, the Duluth Board of Trade, still stands.

Under the watchful eyes of a Red Cross worker (they dressed much like nuns), a girl learned to knit for American soldiers and European refugees in 1918. The World War I effort took place in a shop window in downtown Duluth, on Superior Street. Many youngsters, boys as well as girls, learned to knit garments during the war.

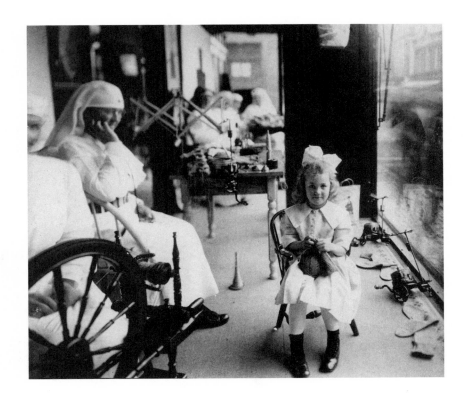

Depression

There were government programs such as the WPA [Works Progress Administration] that gave men work. They did a lot of work around town. I remember homeless men coming to our [Cannon Falls] house begging for something to eat. Mother always found something for them. Some of the buildings at the fair grounds were used as a camp for homeless men.

Rodney Howard Duncan

I know there was a financial depression, but I was protected completely [in St. Paul]. One of my happiest recollections is of my father and my brothers using newspaper coupons, buying five White Castle hamburgers for 10 cents, providing our family of five with three 'burgers each! To this day a White Castle hamburger is a special treat for me, taking me back to our table and the pleasure of family dining! I had no idea, until I was a grown woman, that this was a "depression meal." I still love White Castle burgers and cannot understand my children when they refer to them as "gut bombs."

V. Lynette McKewin Kimble

Northfield Minn.
Nov 25 1932

Gov. F. B. Olsen
State Capitol
St. Paul Minn.
Dear Sir:

You said no man, woman or child need suffer this winter, so I'm going to ask if something can be done for my family. I have been unable to work since May 1st 1932 therefore have no income.

I have a wife and two children, the youngest 12 weeks old. We have no fuel and have not payed rent for six months. The landlord needs his money to pay his taxes.

If you can only help my wife & children, you may forget me. God bless you in Jesus name.

Emanuel C. Jacobsen

P.S. I asked the city to help us. They said they had no funds.
E.J.

The governor wrote back that he was sorry to learn of the destitute circumstances but there was no state fund from which aid could be secured. He suggested consulting the county board to see if it had money: "Some weeks ago the State of Minnesota borrowed a considerable sum of money from the Federal government, which money was allotted to the various counties in need of funds for relief purposes."

Kids at Margaret Playground in St. Paul were given bottled milk in 1938. They're less than ecstatic, but perhaps appreciative. People were hungry during the Great Depression.

Finnish American twins June and Jean Seppala modeled A-line cotton dresses made in Minneapolis on a sewing project of the Works Progress Administration. This was during the Depression, in about 1938.

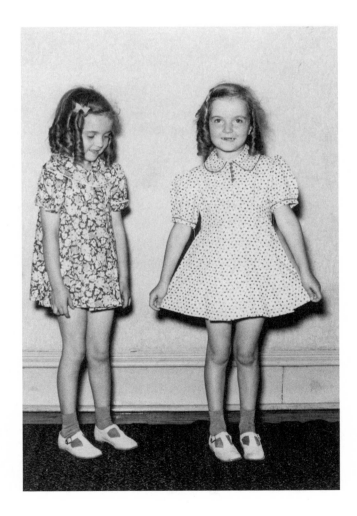

Moms made sleepwear in a Works Progress Administration sewing project at Rice Nursery School, St. Paul, in 1937. Maybe the little one didn't like the jammies with feet.

World War II

On Sunday morning, Dec. 7, 1941, the Japanese bombed Pearl Harbor, destroying a large portion of our nation's Pacific fleet . . . For the first time ever, the very next day, a free-standing big old Philco radio appeared beside the teacher's desk [in our two-room Long Lake grade school]. At the appropriate time, Mrs. Schumann turned it on so we kids could hear "history in the making." Soon the voice of our president, Franklin Delano Roosevelt, was heard declaring war on the Axis powers—Japan, Germany and Italy. Even at age 13, I sensed the world of my childhood was ending, and that the one in which I would spend the rest of my life would be quite different, though I hoped not as sad as for those already fleeing Western Europe and our Pacific outposts.

In our family, our main concern was for a cousin who was in the Navy, stationed aboard the USS *California*. Within a few days, we heard "over the radio" that his ship was one of those badly damaged by the attack on Hawaii. Long-distance phone calls being unknown, we didn't learn until months later, thanks to Western Union [telegraph company] that our cousin, George Feser, had survived by jumping from his ship into the oil-slicked waters of the harbor. Swimming as fast as he could away from the ship, upon reaching shore he hurriedly climbed from the oily black muck, just as it caught fire. He survived, but many of his buddies did not.

In those pre-TV days, newspapers and radio were our chief sources of war news. And so began a 10 P.M. ritual in many Minnesota homes: the

During World War II, children collected aluminum cans and items for the war effort. This group gathered at a Minneapolis streetcar stop in July 1941.

radio was turned on to hear Cedric Adams read the latest news from the Teletype machines. Not until many days later, and then only in our local theatre, could we see the horrendous devastation of our Westernmost naval base on "Movietone News."

Ruth Feser Hale

I remember rationing. It did not seem to be a great hardship, though I think my mother was exceptionally talented at stretching food and making do. She and dad planted a "Victory Garden" on a plot about a mile from our house. Mother, and sometimes Dad, would take the bus down to the garden, hoes and rakes in hand, and spend a few hours tending the garden. In the fall they would take the car to bring home the harvest. From that garden, Mom canned hundreds of quarts of vegetables. She also baked all our bread, made jams and jellies from any fruit that could be picked. We got eggs and some meat from the farm, so we fared well, and the rationing of sugar, meats and some other items did not greatly change our fare. Meals were simple, and we mostly ate all three meals at home together at the family table. My dad would say the "Come Lord Jesus" table prayer before every meal.

Such coordination. Her dress, hat, doll carriage, and dolls' hats all match. This child went all out to collect aluminum for defense needs.

When in school, we kids would usually walk home for lunch which might be cornbread and syrup, Spanish rice, a homemade soup, biscuits and bacon gravy and some leftovers from dinner the night before.

Everything was used, and very little was thrown out.

There wasn't even any garbage pickup. We had a burning barrel out in back by the garage where we burned some papers and whatever else could not be recycled. Everything was saved. I remember that Mother would take the waxed paper out of the cereal boxes, smooth it out, refold it, and use it again. Conservation of everything was not only patriotic, but also practical, as many, many things were in short supply. *We reused, made over, or did without.* Many manufacturing plants that previously produced domestic items had been retooled and were in war production. I recall my mother and grandmother unraveling old sweaters and reusing the yarn to make a new garment . . . Mother would also make coats for my sister and I out of old men's suits. The buttons would be cut off, and the lining would be saved. Our throw-away society now is filling up landfills rapidly. The World War II housewives would not have believed that people could be so wasteful. I think some of us even developed a moral issue out of being saving and careful. Some of the elder pack rats of today come out of the post-depression World War II conservative society.

I think rationing was harder on households that did not grow any of their own food. Ration cards were issued to each family member. These were coupons that were torn out upon purchase of a rationed item. If someone were to come and stay for any length of time, they would be expected to bring their own ration book. Some items, particularly meats, could be bought on the black market. That was under-the-counter kind of selling that would not require coupons, but which would be more expensive. Meats particularly were available "black market." This was probably more true in agricultural areas where food from the farms could be slipped into the city to a profiteer without much danger of reprisals.

Dorothy J. Pederson Nelson, 1940s

Talk of the war was everywhere, and Dad always wanted to listen to the news. [That] night [in Minneapolis, when I was five] was different, and I don't know why. After the blackout, we all went to bed in our usual fashion, but for some reason I could not fall asleep.

My restlessness increased, and so did my imagination. Mom and Dad would help. I went to their bedside, whimpering.

"What's the matter?" Mother asked.

"I don't know," was my response. At that moment I really did not know. But then I started to cry.

"There are Japs under my bed."

"No there aren't. That could never happen," said Dad.

"I'm so scared," I cried. By then I was desperate. And then I became hysterical.

"Please, please help!" I screamed.

My parents quickly went into comfort mode, a little frightened themselves and realizing that constant talk of the war impacted their child, and probably most children. They picked me up and cradled me between them with soothing words until I fell asleep.

Joyce A. (Bosak) Meyer, 1943

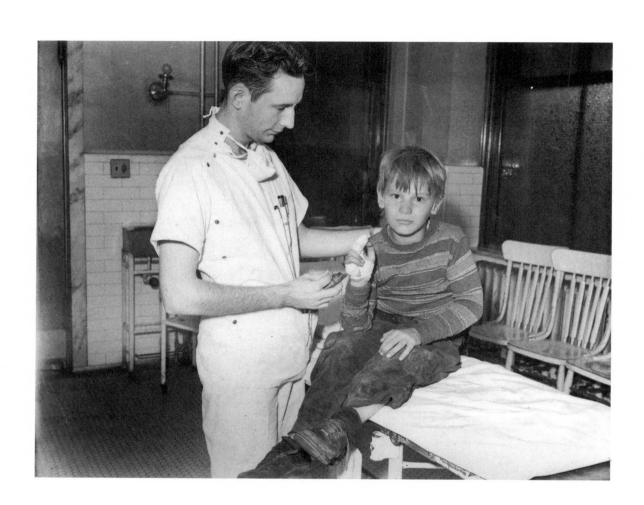

Well-Being

FACING PAGE

A doctor treated a
boy's hand injury in a
Minneapolis hospital's
emergency room in
September 1944.
Those ERs have been
familiar sights to many
a child and parent.

*Imagine a nine-year-old boy suffering a horribly broken leg in 1874, before
anesthesia was widely available. Isaac Haycraft survived that trauma, and so
did many polio patients treated in the mid-1900s by Minnesota's Sister Kenny.
But generations have witnessed and feared epidemics and early deaths and
multiple losses. The historic record shows intense grief.*

Health

*To win immigrants to early Minnesota, promoters stressed its healthful
climate. The 1868 "Guide to Minnesota" flat-out bragged, "The climate is the
principal boast of Minnesota. It is claimed to be 'the healthiest in the world.'
The testimony of thousands of cured invalids, and the experience and statistics
of twenty years, confirm this." The guide told of large numbers of people who
arrived in Minnesota "hopelessly gone with consumption [tuberculosis] or
other chronic disease" and came to enjoy good health here. Children weren't
mentioned, but imagine the relief that harried parents would feel about
bringing young ones to a healthful place.*

*   *   *

*Isaac Haycraft, a southern Minnesota farmer and hog raiser, in 1943 wrote his
reminiscences of his boyhood near Madelia. This story happened in 1874, when
he was nine.*

> It was the custom of the teacher to throw the surplus water from the school
> water pail, when school let out for the day, into these holes [near the corners
> of the schoolhouse], and by doing so the banks of the holes were made a
> rounding glare of ice. I was the first to meet with an accident on this ice. I
> came to the door from inside the building, on the run, the door being open.
> A large boy gave me a violent push, and the first place I struck was this
> slanting glare of ice, and the contact broke my left leg above the knee. Not
> knowing what a broken bone was, I tried to walk, but each time the pain was
> terrific. Sister Eugenia ran home, about a quarter of a mile distant, and told

father and mother what had happened. They hitched the team to the sled and put in a feather bed, to make my ride home more bearable. Sure enough, my leg was broken.

I thought in my ignorance my leg would have to be taken off entirely, but the folks finally convinced me it could be saved. [My brother] Emery struck out for Madelia to get a doctor to set the leg. It was giving me plenty of pain. Doctor Woods was the only doctor at Madelia who could take care of such a fracture. When Em arrived in Madelia, he learned that Doctor Woods was away out in Antrim Township, in Watonwan County, taking care of a German who had gotten mixed up in a stabbing affair.

There was no other way but for Em to drive to Antrim, another 16 or 18 miles, and get the doctor, which he did, arriving home sometime after midnight. Doc looked me over and said "Um" a few times and got busy. He got a board, about three or four inches wide, and sawed three pieces, about 16 or 18 inches long, and nailed them together in box form. Next he made four splints from a new piece of siding. These splints were about one-half inch thick and two or three inches wide and about one foot long. Then he secured a lot of bandages, which were torn from a bed sheet. When all was ready, he told Emery to tie a heavy halter rope to my ankle, on the leg that was broken, and to lie on the floor, on his back, and put his feet against the foot of the bedstead, because he was going to have to do some tall pulling on that leg. Then he stationed father, sitting on the bed with his back to the foot of the bedstead, and told him to place both hands firmly around my leg, where it joined my body, and hold it firmly when Emery began to pull.

Doc explained that the break was slanting and the bone at each end of the break was pointed and sharp, and, inasmuch as I had borne my weight on it trying to walk, I had forced these points into the flesh and caused laceration, hemorrhage and, by that time, inflammation and constricted muscles.

He said it would take a hard pull to get the bones evenly together. He had no anesthetic to give me. He told me to take a big drink of whisky that he had with him, but, no sir, I would not drink any of that stuff. So he said, "Yell, then."

He gave the word for Em to pull, and pull he did. Father put all his strength to his end of the leg. I thought I would die right there, the pain was so severe. It seemed more than a 9-year-old boy could bear. Doc had a large hand and terribly long, strong fingers. He finally got that break together. Mother stood nearby with the splints and bandages and helped Doc get the leg bandaged. Doc said she was as efficient as a graduate nurse. When the leg was bandaged, the pain soon subsided. It was now about 3 o'clock in the morning, and the doctor stayed the rest of the night.

I was forced to lie flat on my back day and night. My leg was strapped in the box that Doc had made. Oh say, but I had nightmares, you bet. Even to this day, if I go to sleep lying on my back, it won't be long until I am in distress . . .

After a few weeks, good old Uncle Andrew Keech, one of our neighbors, brought me a dandy pair of crutches he had made. I was not long in learning how to use them. Soon I was able to bear weight on the broken leg, and within a short time could get out and hobble around. I had a bad limp for quite a while. However, I was keen to get outdoors and whoop it up with my hand sled on the big snow banks and made a rapid recovery. During the time I was confined to the house, mother took a lot of time with me in my studies, and I acquired quite a reputation for spelling. There were spelling contests throughout the whole county in those days.

I trained myself to walk straight, regardless of the handicap. I have been able to engage in all kind of athletics, with average accomplishments. Old Doc Woods did a good job.

*   *   *

To the Editor of the Tribune.

I thought I would write a few words about the croup [an inflammation of the larynx and trachea in children, causing breathing difficulties]. One of my little ones had it last week; we tried everything to make her vomit, but nothing would help her. At last I thought I would try tobacco. I took a piece two inches square and boiled it in vinegar until it all swelled out; then put in a flannel sack and put it on her stomach. It relieved her in less than five minutes. It must not be left on more than 20 minutes. It saved my baby's life. There are so many children who die with the croup, I thought I ought to tell it.

A Farmer's Wife, Hobart, Otter Tail County

[Editor] If the remedy is effectual, it is certainly a cheap and convenient one. We can safely say that the writer of the above is a lady whose integrity is above reproach.

Minneapolis Tribune, January 7, 1883

The mother of the family had to be the doctor, had to be ready to cure diseases and cope with all but the most serious of accidents. Mother knew a lot about practical medicine. She took us through measles, a number of cases of pneumonia, scarlet fever and diphtheria—all without any complications or serious after-effects. I remember this clearly: When a disease hit one of us, we knew it would just go right through the whole family.

How would she do this?

The first thing we'd do was move all the beds from the downstairs into the living room—the living room looked like a battlefield—so mother could

Soap and warm water and a good scrubbing, please. The Phyllis Wheatley House in Minneapolis taught good health habits in about 1920.

keep an eye on us from the kitchen. When one of us got sick, we were popped right into bed. We had to stay in bed where it was warm, and there was no fooling about it.

What medicines did she use?

She knew how to make a number of different teas, each one with its own curative qualities: saffron, senna, sarsaparilla were all used. Castor oil was the common laxative. We had to take it no matter how we protested. Mother also made poultices to draw out infections. She had a home-made cough syrup made out of honey and lemon juice. Flax-seed was used in some poultices, and hot mustard for foot baths. Mother also used to give us pumpkin seeds to eat. I never knew why until I mentioned it one time to Dr. Mary Ghostley. She said, "I can tell you what that was for—worms!"

Mother lived in absolute horror of having an epidemic hit the family. I remember once that a family who lived about half a mile from us had whooping cough. Mother warned us not to go near their house. It was in the summer. One day she stepped to the door, and down the path to our house there came the woman with all her children. Mother met her at the door. "I'm sick and tired of staying home all alone," [the neighbor woman] said. I remember that mother turned to Celia (who was about 16 then) and said, "Take the children and run down by the river and YOU STAY THERE AND PLAY AND DON'T YOU COME BACK!" Then she shooed us out the back door. We had a good time that day. We climbed trees and played games. At noon mother sent the hired man out with a big basket of food for us. We had blankets, all took a nap and in the afternoon we went home. We never did get the whooping cough.

Lillian MacGregor Shaw, 1880s and 1890s

Former governor and U.S. senator Alexander Ramsey was on an anti-smoking crusade for his thirteen-year-old grandson, Alexander Ramsey Furness (known as Ramsey or Alex):

Alexander Ramsey's journal, June 24, 1890: "[I promised my grandson] a dollar if he did not smoke at all when away picnicking at Snail Lake farm tomorrow." And on July 3, 1890: "[My grandson] had promised me not to smoke cigars or tobacco in any shape, pledged me he had not done so. I gave him $1.00."

The grandson, at age sixteen, wrote to his sister Anita on September 11, 1894: "Mama of course had to give me instructions in front of about fifty people at the [train] station, not to smoke or do anything of that sort, and she said it loud enough to be heard at seven corners."

And the next year, December 27, 1895, his mother, Marion Ramsey Furness, wrote to her daughter: "[Ramsey] is awfully sweet, and looks so absurd standing in front of the Library mantle smoking a little pipe.

"[His] Grandpa said the other day to me, 'I smelt tobacco about Alex, do you suppose he smokes?' I said, 'Yes I do, in fact I know he does.' Whereat he seemed

Posed as a bad boy in about 1875, Joseph Henry Sherburne set up props of a bottle, a cigarette or cigar, and a boater hat. His sloppy posture adds the perfect touch.

horrified and indignant, but has said nothing to Ramsey. I told him I deplored it as much as he did, but it wasn't a crime, or even a misdemeanor, and there were many worse things he might do than that."

*   *   *

The next town [that her father served as a Methodist minister] was Sherburn in Martin Co., where I was born July 21, 1896—two months premature. I could fit quite comfortably into a shoebox. Ladies said to my poor little mother, "Oh, I doubt if you'll raise *that* child." How mistaken they were, the tough little thing having lived to be 90. [Actually, she lived to age ninety-two.]

Jo Lutz Rollins, 1896

[One August on an outing] we ate all the muskmelon and watermelon we could eat . . . Was I sick on the way home—too much mixed-up food and all of it wanted to come up. When we got to Anoka, Dad bought some blackberry brandy and made me drink some. It helped. I felt better the rest of the way home . . .

I had so much toothache when I was young. I'd come home from school crying. I'd put a pillow over my head and cry myself to sleep. When I woke up, the toothache was generally gone. Mother took me to the dentist once. I had an abscessed tooth and the dentist put Novocain in three teeth, but the abscessed one hurt so bad when he pulled it that I jumped out of the dentist's chair and wanted to go home and leave the other two teeth. The dentist was very angry at me. Mother persuaded me to have the other two out, and they never hurt a bit to have pulled. The dentist said that he didn't get the pus bag out of the abscessed tooth, so I had to go twice a week and he treated the abscess. I went to the dentist for two months and my face was all swollen. Mother put an onion poultice on my face, and overnight it burst on the outside and it had eaten a hole right through my jaw bone. I missed lots of school because of toothache.

Lena L Borchardt, about 1900

When I was about 7 or 8 years old, I came down with a light case of smallpox. I was bundled into a horse-and-buggy and take to a small hospital on the west side of North Dale Street [in St. Paul]. While I was there, one of the patients called me to a window, pointed out to the yard and said, "That's where they bury the dead ones." Not a pleasant thought for one so young.

Emily Panushka Erickson, about 1907

Thersday Mar 29th 1911

Papa broght hom a nuther bottle of medisen. I had just goten rid of one bottle of Beef Iron and wine and nether of them tast good at all.

Glanville Smith

In the bleak children's ward of St. Mary's Hospital, Minneapolis, in 1924, two little girls were curious about a photographer. In those days, parents couldn't spend the night with patients and visiting hours were short.

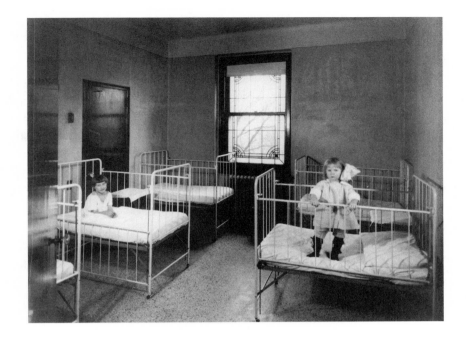

This "hospital" was at Tilden School in St. Paul in 1939. Gender roles ruled. The boy was the doctor, of course, and the girl was the Red Cross nurse.

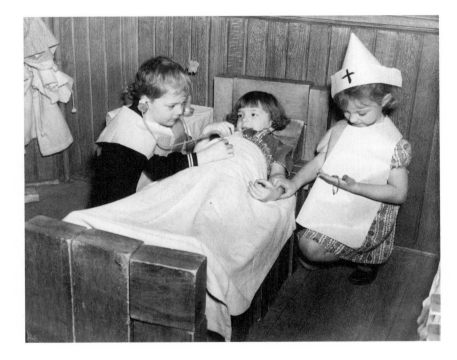

Elsie was a couple years older than we and, no doubt tired of child play, said, "Let's go inside and listen to the grown-ups." This may have cramped their style a bit. The conversation had to be limited to chores and chickens and news items suitable for our tender years. Our family took pains that we should remain as children, ignorant of a few facts of life until the proper time. If a cow was giving birth to a calf, we were forbidden to enter the barn. "Kanske de tar mistanke," was my father's rationale. (Maybe they'll get suspicious.) I knew what he meant because Mildred Nelson had told me when I was 9 years old where babies come from. That year Glen was born, and the next two years Lucille and Milton were born. Each time Papa brought the little bundle in to surprise us, I hated to act surprised, I hated to pretend I believed that the doctor had brought each in his satchel, and I even had to pretend I was pleased so not to spoil Papa's joy. I felt sorry for Mama—all that extra work with another baby. She was so little and thin—if only she had been nice and fat like Mrs. Ed Larson!

Irene Lindahl Krumpelmann, 1910s

If mother is caught shoving baby through the window of the cabinet at the postal station, don't jump to the conclusion that she is mailing the child. Don't assume that baby is in for a parcel post ride, even if the postal clerk is seen weighing the child.

For the St. Paul post office, now "humanized," will weigh babies as well as attend to its usual functions of distributing the mails.

An order issued by Postmaster Charles J. Moos Monday, and effective at the fifty-seven postal substations in St. Paul this morning, instructs all heads of branch officers to be in readiness to weigh the babies of the neighborhood. Knowing accurately the weight of infants is so important a consideration in safeguarding their health that the postmaster regards it an obligation to society to make the office scales available.

St. Paul Pioneer Press, February 14, 1922

Tuberculosis took an especially heavy toll among Minnesota Indians. The state established a sanatorium called Ah-gwah-ching, which operated near Walker from 1907 to 1962.

Sophie [an Ojibwe Indian child] is a glamour lady at the age of six. Accounts of what she does, what she says, what she wears are more eagerly listened to than any Hollywood reporter. She is a slender brunette with a light graceful walk . . .

It happens that she has a room to herself, but not because she wants to be alone as she is the happiest kind of an extrovert. Out of her blanket she will make a doll and for an hour at a time she will sing to this armful. Hers is an unrepressed nature. When she is happy, she sings and laughs loudly, and when she is unhappy, she protests and cries just as loudly.

Sophie has an eccentricity; she does not want her bed tucked in at the end. That, added to the more or less normal dislikes of rest hours and her pleasant singing of Chippewa songs, made her a "personality" at once. And her fame grows every day.

Girls in cute jumpers looked well at the Ponemah Indian Health Camp at Red Lake in Beltrami County in about 1938.

Girls being treated for tuberculosis at Glen Lake Sanatorium in May 1932 didn't wear shirts outside because sunshine was considered healing. Their nurses caps were made of paper. Treatment of the dollies somehow involved eye droppers.

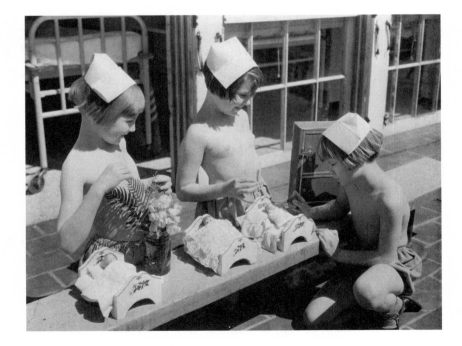

There was the time Sophie was given a pair of rather worn flannel pajamas to wear. She was exceptionally quiet during the following rest hour, but the nurse who opened her door wasn't prepared for what she saw; Sophie, draped in her towels after the fashion of Bali beauties, was sitting on her untouched bed crooning to a family of rag dolls that an hour before were flannel pajamas. The baby doll was in a hammock tied between the rods of the bed-end, and it too had come from the same piece of cloth.

Hardly a day after, nurses came in answer to loud wails from her room. They found her lying on her stomach, feet on the pillows, clutching something in one fist and spitting rosily on a pile of tissues in the middle of the bed. She had just pulled out her first tooth, and no one had ever told her that teeth come out!

The Moccasin, July 1939

Young patients spent time in 1937 at the Lymanhurst Hospital Cardiac Clinic, a branch of Minneapolis General Hospital. This was the boys' ward.

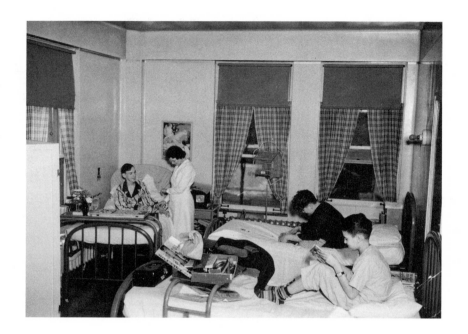

"Please, Sister Kenny, will you help my child." In the 1940s, letter after anguished letter to Elizabeth Kenny pleaded for help. For generations, polio was known as the dreaded killer and crippler of childhood, and in the 1940s Sister Kenny at her Minneapolis headquarters offered the best hope for recovery.

Sister Kenny was neither a Catholic nor a nun. In British countries, including her native Australia, "sister" was the title for a head nurse. But Sister Kenny was not the trained nurse she claimed to be; she was largely self-taught. Without accreditation but with great enthusiasm, she went to work as a nurse in the Australian bushland.

In 1911 she encountered her first case of polio, then called infantile paralysis. Not knowing how to treat it, she improvised. Sister Kenny didn't realize it, but her treatment was the exact opposite of what the medical establishment around the world did for polio victims. What was believed to be right was immobilizing affected limbs in splints, casts, and braces as a way of limiting the polio virus's damage to muscles. Patients were kept flat and quiet. Children were taken to operating rooms and had their limbs straightened under anesthesia. They woke up screaming.

Sister Elizabeth Kenny demonstrated her therapy techniques—including gentle manipulation of limbs—in about 1942.

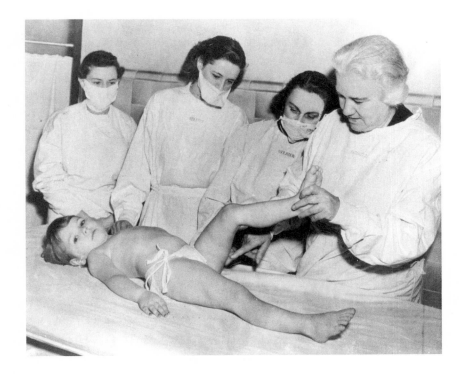

All wrong, Sister Kenny insisted. She deduced that polio made muscles inflamed and weak. They needed moist heat and movement. She never claimed to cure polio, just to restore damaged bodies.

Even in Australia, most doctors rebuffed her. Yet in 1940, some Australian medical men urged her to visit the United States to have her idea scientifically investigated. Turned away by doctors in California and New York (one of whom told her bluntly that no U.S. doctor would be interested and to go back to Australia), she was greeted with respect at the Mayo Clinic and the University of Minnesota Hospitals. She started to train students in 1941 at General Hospital in Minneapolis and at the university. So amazing were the results that Minnesotans opened her Kenny Institute on December 17, 1942. Minneapolis became the world's center for polio treatment.

Letters of thanks and despair poured in from all over the world.

Dec. 3, 1942
1707 Stevens Ave. So., Mpls.

Dear Sister Kenny,

I would like to call your attention to the case of our little girl, Marlene Cook. She was under treatment for Polio at the General Hospital, with a new treatment, back in May 1940. We were called down to the hospital & asked if we would be willing to submit Marlene to the treatment you were using. We had been told that Marlene would be crippled all of her life . . . She was stricken when she was 14 months old. We talked it over & figured to grasp at every straw to get her cured, so she was one of the first ten children that had the privilege of taking your treatment in Mpls., & no doubt the U.S.

When she left the hospital, she took treatments from the Curative Work Shop, & in a short time was considered completely cured . . .

I was sending a picture along, taken at the General Hospital when Marlene was 2 yrs. 4 mo. It might refreshen your memory to whom we are talking about. Would you please return it, as we haven't any other picture of her at that time.

Sincerely . . ,

Mr. and Mrs. D. C. Cook

Jan. 2nd 1943

Los Angeles, Calif.

Dear Sister Kenny,

. . . Our one and only child, a boy of fourteen, was stricken with Polio. They say he was a pre-paralytic case, but I feel sure that if they had used the old method of treatment on him, he might have developed paralysis during such treatment. The General Hospital here had begun using your technique only a few months before our Glenn was brought in . . . When he was first taken to the hospital, his dad and I could hardly look at each other without bursting into tears. All we could think of then was the twisted body of our boy, who had begun growing into manhood with such a beautiful body and so good-looking. Could anyone have blamed us.

So many thanks to our good God, and then to you, Sister Kenny. We shall never forget to remember you in our prayers.

Our boy is back home. The final check-up shows he is perfect . . . It is a wonderful world, after all.

Sincerely,

Mrs. Esther Ciarfeo

P.S. Oh yes, since being in the hospital, Glenn has made up his mind to become a doctor.

Monday, Jan. 18, 1943

New York City, New York

Dear Sister Kenny,

. . . Will you please send us a picture of your self to us, not a costly one, any one would do. It would seem like a small fortune to us to own one, so we could put it in a place of honor in our home. And I know Kenneth would love that so when he got older he could see the face of one he could thank from the bottom of his heart. [You] made him walk again.

Thanking you again.

Kenneth's mother,

Mrs. Fred Zigrest

Parker, Arkansas
March 13, 1944

Dear Sister Kenny,

. . . I am now a perfect normal 16 year old boy with the ambition to become a actor and singer. And I hope that someday I will succeed, as you have in your great work. I remember the little boy next to me in the hospital sometimes. He was never to walk again. Then I feel wonderful because at last we have someone in the world to cure the desease that has wrecked so many lives. I know now that it wasn't a mirecal, like the doctors said, that healed me. It was the magic touch of God massaging my legs . . .

Yours Most Respectfully,

Charles Martin

Western Union telegram:

ON 26TH OCTOBER 1945 SIXTEEN MONTHS OLD BABY DAUGHTER DIAGNOSED INFANTILE PARALYSIS STOP VERY GRATEFUL FOR ANY HELP YOU CAN OFFER STOP PREPARED TO DO ANYTHING TO CURE DAUGHTER PLEASE CABLE REPLY JACOB RUBIN NO 1 BIALIK STREET HAIFA PALESTINE

This letter was typed. Almost all the others were handwritten.

May 19, 1947
Reno, Nevada

Dear Sister Kenny,

I would be very happy if you would send me your autograph. If you have a picture of yourself please send me one. I am 9 years old and in the 3rd grade. I like to type very much.

Sincerely Yours,

Garth Sibbald

Letter writers begged Sister Kenny for help for everything from palsy to blindness. Her secretary often had to respond that Sister was sorry but her help could be given only to patients in an acute phase of polio. Meanwhile, Sister Kenny kept pushing for changes in medicine—some good, some bad. Seldom diplomatic, she made terrible enemies, mostly in the medical community.

But Sister Kenny had no trouble winning over the public. She rode victorious in the Aquatennial parade in 1944, just four years after she showed up in Minneapolis. For ten years American women named her one of the women most admired, second only to Eleanor Roosevelt, in the Gallup Poll.

Sister Kenny herself was on hand to celebrate the Kenny Institute's first birthday with young polio patients in December 1943. Because of her, Minneapolis became the world's premier polio-treatment center.

An exuberant patient: Peter F. Schroeder demonstrated his dexterity to his mother, Ruth, in their St. Cloud home in 1948. He had been successfully treated for polio at the Kenny Institute.

She was diagnosed with Parkinson's and in 1951 returned to Australia. She died in her hometown at about age seventy-two (she gave various birth dates) the next year. Shortly before her death, she was the most admired in the Gallup Poll.

A major financial scandal damaged the institute's reputation after her death. Fund-raisers went to prison. With the development of the Salk and Sabin polio vaccines, polio was virtually eliminated as a disabling disease in the United States by the 1960s. But Sister Kenny's principles of muscle "reeducation" proved beneficial in treating other crippling disorders. The Sister Kenny Institute carries on in Minneapolis, an acute-care rehabilitation center.

*   *   *

Epidemic years for polio were 1940, 1944, 1945, and 1946. Sister Kenny worked with children, and adults, who had active polio cases. Her 1948 brochure gave these numbers of reported cases in Minnesota, North and South Dakota, Iowa, and Wisconsin:

Year	Cases
1932	275
1933	611
1934	343
1935	258
1936	190
1937	931
1938	158
1939	917
1940	1,816
1941	488
1942	235
1943	624
1944	1,112
1945	1,255
1946	5,651
1947	693

Death

Alexander and Anna Ramsey's firstborn child, Alexander Jenks Ramsey, known as Sonny, died in St. Paul in 1850, probably of fever, at the age of three. His father, then the first governor of the Minnesota Territory, wrote in his journal:

Sunday 28th, About 12 at midnight our dear boy sunk very sensibly, and being called [the doctor] applied restoratives [medicine] & he shortly recruited [was somewhat better].

But about 5 ½ AM he expired without a groan—Oh my God how bitter is the cup. Give myself and poor wife strength to drink the dregs. Never, never did I conceive that there could be such a weight of affliction laid upon a poor mortal. The only consolation a stricken heart can find is that our lovely boy has gone to a "world of Glory."

Alexander Ramsey was governor of Minnesota when this portrait was taken in about 1850 with his son, Alexander Ramsey Jr. When the boy died at age three, Ramsey wrote in grief, "Never, never did I conceive that there could be such a weight of affliction laid upon a poor mortal."

Only eighteen months later, the Ramseys' second son, William Henry, died at age nineteen months. Their third child, Marion, survived into adulthood.

*   *   *

Feb. 20, 1863

When I was going past the ditch that goes through the marsh I saw Frank Gregory. He told me to go and look in the ditch—in one of the branches. I expected to see a dead dog or something like that, but instead I saw the body of a dead baby! It was very young, as if it was just born. It was in a corn sack, & naked! Frank Gregory said it was a girl. I suppose some woman had a baby & didn't want it, so she put it in a sack & let it freeze to death out there!

Frederick Allis

From the 1872 diary of Lewis Johnson, a thirty-four-year-old Goodhue County farmer:

Saturday, Nov. 2. I was over to see Chr's [brother Christian's] baby she is sick.

Sunday, Nov. 3. I went to Red Wing on Horseback after Doctor Jahnig for Chr's baby. I came home in the evening bro't more Medicine for Chr's baby.

Thursday, Nov. 7. Chr. baby is still very sick.

Saturday, Nov. 9. Chr's baby very low at present.

Mary Lommel, the eighteen-month-old daughter of Joseph P. and Anna Lommel of Albany, died October 28, 1907, and is shown here in her coffin, a rosary threaded through her fingers and a crown of flowers on her head. She appears so well that probably she died suddenly; maybe diphtheria took her. Photographs of deceased persons were common in an era when mourners from far away couldn't get to funerals.

Sunday, Nov. 10. Chr's child, Carrie Ella, Died this morning about 6 o'clock 1 year 2 mos & 5 days old I think disease Dropsy on the Brain & Inflamation of Stomach.

Monday, Nov. 11. Bro't out Coffin & other things ready for the funeral tomorrow. Mrs. Mary Gorton came along home to help about the burryal.

Tuesday, Nov. 12. Buried Carrie Ella, Chr's and Emma's only child, in the grave-yard near the Presbyterian Church of Goodhue. Revs. Borgerson & Lindquist attended & Rice's, Danielson's & Terkelson's & our own Families attended the funeral; in all 6 teams [of horses] and 30 person's.

At the end of each year's diary, Lewis wrote a meticulous account of everything spent during the year. For November 11: Coffin Chr's Carrie. $6.00

*   *   *

In the spring of 1878, typhoid fever entered our home [in Vasa]. I do not know of any other home in our community that was affected. Sister Emma, [me] Eva and [brother] Lawrence became patients. Dr. Brynildsen (a Norwegian) had just located in Vasa. It was said he had failed to pass the State Board, so had never put out his shingle. He established himself in the grocery business and called on sick people also. He was our attending physician.

Emma was very ill and remarked to mother, "Poor Eva, if she will be as sick as I am." I suffered many relapses, and it was summer before I was out of bed. Lawrence recovered very quickly. The day Emma was taken ill, she attended the funeral of Oscar Swanson, a neighbor, 19 years old, who died from T.B. As they proceeded to the cemetery, she stopped off, being too sick to go farther.

Emma passed away on Good Friday in the bloom of youth. She was a beautiful child with mother's blue eyes and blonde hair. She possessed a sweet disposition, kind and gentle in all of her ways, aged fourteen and a half years. The day of her burial was rainy, and in those days the funeral service was conducted beside the open grave. Mother was very tired and caught cold, which resulted in a cough with which she struggled all of the rest of her life.

Eva Tilderquist

My sister Betty was born within the year after their marriage [in 1881]. About two months before the second baby, Katy, was born, Betty died of meningitis. Then a few months before Anson was born, Katy died the same way. Milk was so unhygienically handled in those days, and this and teething and wrong ideas of feeding that prevailed then were probably responsible. When Anson was born [in 1884], he was a sickly little thing, and Mother and Father hadn't the faintest hope he would live. They watched over him and every breath he drew, hardly daring to believe he would get through his second summer, which was considered the critical time.

Anson lived! And his sister, Margaret Jackson Bovey, was born in 1887.

*   *   *

These parents, Christian and Mary Holbeck, lived in Morken Township in Clay County, on the border of North Dakota. If they look especially stern or sad in this photo (facing page), probably taken in 1886, there's good reason: three of their children had died of scarlet fever in March 1885, two on the same day. And that's not all the misery. Another five of their children died between 1882 and 1889, making a total of eight in a little more than seven years.

According to a family history of Hans and Johanna Jensen, neighbors of the Holbecks, written later, "Then there was the terrible diphtheria [actually scarlet fever] epidemic ... Only one country doctor and almost all the families in the neighborhood lost some or all of their children. It was almost impossible to get help, as people were afraid of that dreaded disease. A neighbor, Mrs. Holbeck, told Mrs. Jensen if she and her husband lost all of their children, they couldn't bear it. A few days later their children became ill. Mrs. Jensen sat with the Holbeck children at night to relieve the parents. One night Mr. Holbeck had made a coffin for one of their children and went to the Concordia cemetery in [nearby] Moland Township for burial, when he returned another child had

Holbeck family
portrait

died . . . The Jensens were one of the fortunate families, both of their children were spared."

Here's a list of the Holbeck children who succumbed:

Elmer Victor, died June 4, 1882, age one year, eight months, cause: unknown. (Not an uncommon listing on death certificates of the period.)

Einar Victor, June 20, 1884, two days, cause of death is blank.

Claudine, July 2, 1884, one year, seven months, cause: teething.

William, March 2, 1885, six years, scarlet fever.

Axel, also March 2, 1885, three years, four months, scarlet fever.

Wilhelmina, March 20, 1885, thirteen years, scarlet fever.

Huld, September 20, 1885, three months, six days, cholera.

Willis, October 20, 1889, three years, croup.

Their remaining four children, shown here, survived to adulthood. They are, left to right, Dagmar, Agnes, Herman, and Walter. Walter died of alcoholism at age twenty-eight.

*　　*　　*

In 1889, Alpheus Beede Stickney's grandson, named for him, died. Stickney wrote to his son Sam, the child's father, that grief for a deceased child never ends.

The Grand Pacific Hotel
Chicago, Ill.
Dec. 26, 1889

My dear children,

I have just this moment learned of the death of your darling little boy. Words are not at my command to express the sorrow I feel at the loss of my little pet, nor sympathy for you both in this great affliction.

Your mother and I have been most fortunate with our children, but the loss of our dear little Edith [at the age of about ten months, in 1871, eighteen years previously] has never been effaced from my memory. Although time has soothed the keen anguish, it is still a sacred memory which we could not forget if we would and would not if we could.

The death of dear little Alpheus to you must be almost crushing. I pray that you may have strength to bear it and that as time passes by it may be a new and sacred bond which shall bind your two souls together in, if possible, a higher and more enduring love than ever before.

Be assured my dear son and my dear daughter that my most heartfelt sympathy is with you. I hope you will do everything in your power to preserve each other's health and to gradually rise above this most crushing blow.

I shall go home tonight or tomorrow. I hope Sam will not think it necessary to return as long as his absence can be of any service whatever to my dear Charlotte.
Yours with very great love and sympathy,
A. B. Stickney

J. C. "Buzz" Ryan, who went on to become a well-known forest ranger near Duluth, was about seven years old when his older brother Halbert, about eight, died in a spinal meningitis epidemic in 1907. As an adult, he told historian Barbara Sommer: "I watched out the upstairs window as my mother walked toward the house after attending the funeral. Several women who were in the house taking care of the other children ran out to tell her the news of the death of another of her children. It was my little sister, Evelyn, who was about two. My mother fell face down on the lawn in front of the house in grief, her arms spread out to her sides."

It is not unthinkable that soon old age will be the chief cause of death, and of sickness there need be very little. It would astonish one to learn that our former generation was much cut off long before old age, by preventable disease. As to my people, mother died of dysentery at 30, father of consumption [tuberculosis] at 49, [first] stepmother Fannie at 34 of the same, [second] stepmother Hattie of rheumatism at about 48, and likely I would have died young of consumption if it had not been for Minnesota and a lucky program for work and hygiene that helped me to overcome a tubercular infancy.

Walter Stone Pardee, about 1920

Irene Lindahl Krumpelmann was eleven when her beloved grandmother died.

The big flu epidemic reach[ed] Clear Lake [Wisconsin] in 1920. In our six years there, my grandparents had never been ill. At 77, Grandma was still making pancakes every morning. On a February morning, as she ladled batter into the seven circlets of the iron griddle brought from Sweden, she began to totter and fell into Papa's arms. The flu turned into pneumonia—and she was gone. No longer would we be shouting to her. No more taking turns churning butter and drinking the delicious buttermilk. No more bringing rounds of butter topped with a rose imprint to a neighbor. Ethel would miss the 25 cents helping Grandma clean house.

And for Grandpa, she had been the light of his life. For years she had been his eyes (I suspect he had cataracts), as she read daily for him from the big Swedish Bible and the weekly *Svenska Amerikaneren* and *Veckoblade* . . .

Uncle Charlie had arrived from Duluth, Aunt Emily from Two Harbors, and Aunt Abbie from the adjoining farm . . . Papa and Uncle Charlie had to dig their own mother's grave, as so many people had the flu. Dear Papa, that very day of the funeral, one of his best friends died, young Albert Carlson. This news so shocked the neighborhood that Louis Benson forgot to toll the bells for Grandma, to Grandpa's chagrin as he had contributed to their purchase. The men wore black arm-bands and the ladies voluminous black veils over their hats and faces. Pauline Larson at the old organ played "Narmare Gud til Dig" (Nearer My God to Thee), most sorrowful of funeral hymns and enough to squeeze tears out of turnips. I felt then, at the age of 11, I could never bear to lose anyone in my family.

Only three weeks later, Grandpa died—of pneumonia and maybe a broken heart.

Learning

FACING PAGE
Sharing the joy of
reading: a child,
father, and mother
(she in a visiting dress)
shared a book in
about 1900.

Our hearts go out to little Fannie, who had to recite "The Highwayman" to the whole school assembly. Gulp! Yet education, we all know, is more than school work. It's plunking on the piano, writing a thank-you note for a necktie ("just the thing I wanted"), and soaking up kindnesses to pass along someday.

Education

My father, Edward Robert Pond, was born at Lake Harriet March 17, 1840 . . . Both Father and Mother [Mary Frances Hopkins Pond, born at Lac Qui Parle in 1843] learned to read while very young. One winter when Father was three and one-half years old, he stayed at Uncle Samuel's [Samuel Pond, an influential missionary to the Indians] while his folks went to Connecticut. He used to tell how he had to stand on a bench because he didn't read as well as Uncle Samuel thought he should. Mother learned to read at the age of three, and before she was four her father bought her a nice leather-covered reference Bible which I still have. When her mother objected saying it was too expensive for a child of that age, her father said as long as she could read it, she should have a good Bible.

The family policy with the Hopkins was that the children were to keep away from the Indians entirely as the Indians were undesirable and should not mingle with them. Father, on the contrary, was taught that the Indians were just as good as anyone else. His only playmates were Indians, and he could speak the Indian language just as fluently as he could English.

Harold H. Pond

In 1854 on [Winona's] Front street about 300 feet east of the railroad bridge was a school of sunburned, bare-footed, one-suspendered doughnut-eaters, presided over by a lady whose name is to memory lost. She wore glasses gracefully and "made good." She landed on the craniums of the youth with the map of every place and the multiplication table set to music. Her sweet voice and pleasant smile tastes good after these long years.

In '54 Winona grew like a mushroom, and Miss Almeda Twitchell came to bat; she fought the main springs of deviltry in the youth of that day. She had a hard job . . . Fifty, or at times more, unruly fighters and their sisters

The Dublin School in Winona County's St. Charles, probably an early spring in the 1950s. By that time, the style of posing for a photograph had changed dramatically and all were expected to smile widely.

had to be shown the road to civilization. Almeda did not have time to spare to crimp her locks [of hair] or play with the powder puff.

The Winona Daily Republic, April 2, 1912

Dec 6, 1860

Here is my school composition: "Description of learning to skate"

First you work half an hour to get your skates on. Then you get up and stand on the ice. Then you begin to shiver till your knees crack by their hitting together so hard. Perhaps some generous fellow will come shoving and push you over to wake you up and half break your head. You get up with no little trouble and being to shiver again. Then again perhaps some kind fellow will come along and begin titting you how to learn to skate. He will probably talk so fast that you can't understand anything. But he will poke his legs about in all directions and tell you to do the same, all this time you will be shivering and shaking and your knees abreaking. Then he goes away and you begin to practice his lessons, thinking it is a very easy thing to learn to skate. So you slide out one leg on purpose and the other sticks out without any help, and they both slide out without any help and the question depends on your bottom whether you are hurt or not. If it is rather soft you can get up without much injury, but if it is hard you either hurt yourself or break a hole in the ice and get wet. This is your first skate. You then get up and stand still a little while but being a little roused to action by your late feat you make another trial. When feet start out in opposite directions stretching your breeches mightily till they rip. Second skate. You again proceed more carefully moving about by inches while the crowds are attracted by a white flag flying from the rip in your breeches till you suddenly fall on your face and smash your nose. This is third skate. Then you get up and stand still till some girl or lady watching the boys skating exclaims, "See that boy is losing his pocket handkerchief out of his pocket." He turns around sudden and sticks his hand around behind him and sure enough his shirt flap is out half way down to his heels. Your betting that you got in your first skate now begins to opperate so you retire. This ends the first day of learning to skate!

Frederick Allis got to be a good skater and spent many happy hours on the ice.

Very early, the Indian boy assumed the task of preserving and transmitting the legends of his ancestors and his race. Almost every evening a myth, or a true story of some deed done in the past, was narrated by one of the parents or grandparents, while the boy listened with parted lips and glistening eyes. On the following evening, he was usually required to repeat it. If he was not an apt scholar, he struggled long with his task; but, as a rule, the Indian boy is a good listener and has a good memory, so that the stories were tolerably well mastered. The household became his audience, by which he was alternately criticized and applauded.

Charles Eastman, 1860s

Sept. 22, 1862
I began school again at Lasher's last Monday. I study Spelling, Reading, Grammar, Natural history, German Grammar and Reading, Anatomy and Physiology. Today I took lessons in all but Nat. Hist. The principal things I lernt lately is: Osteology an account of the skeleton of the Human body. Myology an account of the muscles. Splanchnology an account of the nutritive organs. Angiology an account of the circulating system of arteries and veins. Pneumonology an acct. of the respiratory, vocal, calorific organs. Ichrology an acct. of the lymphatic and secretive system. Neurology an acct. of the Nervous system.

Frederick Allis

It has never been accounted for, and probably never will be, why a boy who will eat four meals, play ball for three hours, gorge himself with unripe fruit,

A fifth-grade classroom at the state public school in the Owatonna orphanage in about 1902 held a variety of ages and races. Children were educated there before they were placed for adoption. There were lots more boys than girls; maybe girls were more easily adoptable.

and go in swimming six times a day during vacation and be healthier than a tombstone, will be seized with all sorts of maladies the very moment the school bell rings.

St. Paul Pioneer Press, October 2, 1875

As much as we all deprecate the too-prevalent use of slang, one cannot help noticing that the later style of expressions of that nature is a tendency, in case the injunction are observed, to cause the person addressed to brace up and have a little more style about him. As witness the following, "Pull down your vest." "Buckle up your under lip." And "Untangle your eyelash."

Stillwater Gazette, June 21, 1876

The Evening Schools have, during the past week, been attended by 848 persons, as compared to 776 persons during the corresponding period of last year. The majority are Scandinavians, and our Swedish boys and girls can certainly never find a better way to spend their time than to attend the schools and receive free instruction in the language of the country.

Translated from *Svenska Amerikanska Posten*, January 26, 1892

A CLEVER SWEDISH GIRL. The newspaper "The Minneapolis Times" had recently arranged a contest among the younger of the grade-school children in the city, and offered a prize of $10.00 for the best written composition. No less than 4,200 compositions were entered for the prize with a composition entitled "The Rabbit." Maria is the youngest daughter of Mr. John Anderson of 35 East Side Flats. She was born in 1881 and came with her parents to this country from Sweden 4 years ago, and neither she nor her parents could then understand a word of English. She has attended American schools since that time, but it must be considered remarkable that a child who only 4 years ago knew nothing about English could win such a contest among such a great number of contestants.

Translated from *Svenska Amerikanska Posten*, December 27, 1892

The nation's first library room especially for children was at the downtown Minneapolis Public Library at Tenth and Hennepin. Already in 1892, several hundred children's books were grouped in a basement corridor as an experiment to get crowding and commotion away from adult patrons. By 1893, all children's books were grouped there. True, children's collections had existed in other libraries, but this is said to be the first with a designated attendant and open shelves for children to browse and find books to take home. When a library wing was added in 1906, the children's collection moved to a newly decorated room on the ground floor.

Children visited a Minneapolis Public Library bookmobile on May 26, 1952. The children's books were conveniently stowed on the lower shelves.

I think you're a very foolish little girl not to spend your spare time on classics, etc., instead of trashy silly stories.

Anita Furness, writing to younger sister Laura

In 1901, ten Sunday School boys of Westminster Presbyterian Church in downtown Minneapolis compiled a "Book of Remembrance." They wrote about their own lives, inserted their photos, and told what their faith meant to them. They updated their account several times, and in 1912 the then grown men added a stack of letters, bound with sealing wax, to be opened by the last survivor. (Whoever that was didn't go back to open the package.) Here's part of what Karl Bowne Raymond wrote at the age of twelve:

After years of instruction, three boys at Our Lady of Guadalupe Church on St. Paul's west side, including Kenneth Garcia (left) and Michael Medina (middle) were ready for the confirmation service. It was probably the 1940s.

I was born Aug the 11 1888 in the city of Minneapolis. My first name is from my father and my second the maiden name of my grandmother. My home has allways been in Minneapolis. When I was about five years old, I entered the Westminster S.S. and have attended there every since . . .

I wood like to see the sights in New York city sometime. I wood like to be a busness man. And intend to save my money so I can own the business. I will use my money for some good purpose. Written this 17 of May 1901

Two years later he wrote,

Sometime I hope to have enough money so as to help the Y.M.C.A. work in the U.S. Navy. And if I had ten thousand dollar to give away, I would give to hospitals $1,000, to foriegn missions $4,000, to home missions $1,000, caring for aged ministers $2,000, Sunday school work $1,000. I would not give any to the librarys or collages because the state could aid them. May 21, 1903

By age nineteen, Karl Raymond knew he wanted to make recreation his life work. The 1941 Who's Who in Minnesota *listed him as the Minneapolis recreation director. Whether or not he ever got his million dollars is not recorded.*

*   *   *

Wanda's first years at school were not altogether happy. School was a strange place where the teachers didn't always understand—for Wanda was a dreamer. Time and again, she would be lost in her own thoughts. At home, when she was unaware of what was going on around her because her thoughts were far away, her father would often say: "Na, my little Wanda is dreaming again!" But Wanda knew that while he teased her affectionately about this tendency to dream, he was actually proud of it. It was, after all, the big dreamer talking to the little one, and a part of the deep bond between them.

Alma Scott, recalling Wanda Gág, who attended school at the turn of the twentieth century

Wanda Gág of New Ulm, who grew up to be a famous author of children's stories, including the 1928 *Millions of Cats,* was a dreamy small child in about 1896.

Fifty years ago—sixty certainly—there was not a pupil nor a public school in Minnesota. The last report showed the total number of scholars enrolled to be 412,671, the value of school houses and sites $17,604,636 and the annual payment on account of teachers' wages $4,347,354.

Brown County Journal, New Ulm, December 13, 1902

Our teacher became ill soon after school [in Turtle River] started in the fall, and a substitute teacher by the name of Finnigan, a tall, nervous man, was hired. He was not a teacher in any way and was too nervous to be around children. The following incident brought an end to his teaching after about a month. Two of the older boys had been caught smoking in the wood shed. They were called to the front of the room where their punishment was to be a whack on the bare hand with a ruler. One of the boys' older sister was afraid her brother might strike the teacher and called out for him to take the punishment. After he had taken his punishment without batting an eye, the sister, Ethel Porter, was called up front by the teacher who was angered by her calling out to her brother. She was told to hold out her hand. She pulled back a little and the teacher struck her across the thumb, breaking it. Ethel fled out the door and home crying. Her mother, a widow, was the janitor of the school. After the room had settled down, Mrs. Porter was seen approaching the school. She was quite a large woman and I believe about 45 years old. As she entered school and strode up the aisle towards the teacher, we noticed a "blacksnake" horsewhip she carried in her hand. Mr. Finnigan arose as she came up the aisle, and she hit him across the face with the whip. He ran from the desk to behind the stove, but she continued to lay on the whip. We children all ran out of the room, and when Mrs. Porter had finished with the whipping, she came out crying and said, "I don't think there will be any more school today." We did not have any school for a week, and a one-armed telegrapher from the depot by the name of Flemmings took over and held classes until our regular teacher returned.

J. C. "Buzz" Ryan, 1909

Problem.—If a student can solve twenty problems in Arithmetic in two and one-half hours, how much pleasure can he find in the same length of time at 1109 5th Ave. S., Fargo, beginning at 7:30 Saturday evening, December tenth, 1910?

Miss Anderson and Miss Nelson will be happy to assist you in solving the above problem.

Historical and Cultural Society of Clay County, 1910

I don't remember when I learned to read. It seems that I always could. I couldn't write, but yes, I could read. When I was in second grade [in Minneapolis], [older brother] Mikie was upstairs in a class that was studying

That shoe tying lesson called for concentration at a Ramsey County nursery school in October 1937. "Stockings" of the time were always baggy.

poetry. He had a small book that had World War I poems in it. The print was the right size for me to read, and the borders on the pages were wide enough for Mikie to doodle his comic-page characters, which he shared with me.

It was during one of our sharing sessions that he let me read from his book. One particular poem was "The Highwayman" [by Alfred Noyes], which fascinated me. I don't know how many times I read it or how long it took me to memorize the entire poem, but one morning in my class Mrs. Groble mentioned poetry. Without thinking I raised my hand and said, "I know a poem." The next thing I knew, I was in front of the class reciting, "The highwayman came riding, up to the old inn-door . . ." I recited the entire work, and then I sat down. Mrs. Groble was so impressed, she took me by the hand and walked me over to the other second-grade room where she asked Miss Amundson if I could recite for her class. Again I went through my shtick, a little bewildered about all the fuss. That afternoon my teacher sent a note home with me, asking if it would be all right if I performed at the school assembly to be held the next day.

The assembly bell rang and all the students and teachers gathered in the gym. Everybody sat on the floor, according to grades kindergarten through third, and we formed rows in front of the stage. The fourth- through the sixth-grade classes sat in back of the little ones. The teachers sat on chairs.

There were several selections performed before me and then it happened. I was led on stage and introduced very properly. I made one mistake: I looked up and saw hundreds of faces of kids and teachers . . . It happened!

For generations, the first day of school has been a picture-taking event. This one is from about 1930.

What happened? Nothing. Nothing. Mrs. Groble and Miss Amundson each coaxed and gave me cues. Finally, I was physically lifted off the stage. I remember going to the bathroom, and my pink bloomers were wet. I remember running home crying. And I do know for a fact that I never appeared in a school performance again.

Fannie S. Schanfield, 1920s

Mother had wanted to send [my brother George, a year ahead of me at University High School] to St. Paul Academy . . . SPA was the preparatory school where "rich boys" went; girls went to Summit School. But when Mother went to the headmaster at SPA with George's grades, he didn't look at them. He just said that he already had one Jewish boy in that class so he couldn't take another. Our dinner table discussion about this was a mixture of anger and resignation; my parents weren't surprised at the rejection.

They knew that the "best" colleges restricted Jewish enrollment; that made it easier for prep schools like St. Paul Academy to deny admission to Jews. At U High, whose faculty included many Ph.D. candidates, I recall only one Jewish faculty member during my six years there. Few colleges and universities would hire Jews; many would not admit us to their graduate programs. Public universities technically did not have policies of discrimination, but individual department heads could be discouraging, especially if the job market realistically offered no place for a Jew.

Ruth F. Brin, about 1930

A BOY'S ESSAY ON GEESE

Geese is a low heavy-set bird which is mostly meat and feathers. His head sits on one side and he sits on the other. Geese can't sing much on account of the dampness of the moistures. He ain't got no between his toes and he's got a little balloon in his stomach to keep him from sinking.

Some Geese when they get big has curls on their tails and is called Ganders. Ganders don't have to sit and hatch, but just eat and loaf and go swimming. If I was a geese, I'd rather be a gander.

[By] C.E.

Cook County News-Herald, May 9, 1935

Two well-dressed boys—one pouty, the other diligent—read *Another Brownie Book* in about 1910.

Generations of guys have known that comics are the best way to practice their reading skills. Here's a newsstand in a drugstore in about 1947.

JOKE: The class had been asked to write an essay on winter, and before they began the teacher gave them a few hints. He suggested that they might introduce a short paragraph on migration. One pupil's attempt read as follows: "In winter it is very cold. Many old people die in winter, and many birds also go to a warmer climate."

The Moccasin, August 1942

Indian Boarding Schools

From the 1880s through the Depression years of the 1930s, thousands of Native American children were removed from their homes and sent, some far away, to boarding schools, supposedly to "civilize" them and remove all traces of "Indianness." Most children sent off to boarding school were twelve or older, but some were as young as six or seven. The idea was to prepare young Indians for citizenship, teach them English, and provide them with a practical, vocational education.

However, the children were treated harshly. For speaking their tribal languages, they were beaten or locked in school jail. They suffered from malnourishment (fresh fruit and vegetables were rarely served) and sometimes severe food shortages and even starvation. Dormitories often were overcrowded, worn down, and disease-infested.

Forced to spend long hours working in the schools' farms and gardens, the children found that little of the harvest got to their tables. Soap was scarce, an investigation found, and even toilet paper was absent from half the facilities inspected. Privacy was unknown. Homesickness and illness—either of the student or of a relative—were considered poor excuses for home visits. Rebellion led many to run away.

Historian Brenda J. Child wrote of Mrs. Isabella Strong of the Red Lake Reservation begging the Flandreau superintendent to allow her "terribly homesick" daughter, Claudia, to visit home in 1938. Isabella wrote, "It seems it would be much easier to get her out of prison than out of your school."

Yet, during the Depression, some Indian communities were so poverty-stricken that they gratefully sent children to the boarding schools.

*   *   *

Way Quah Gishig (Snow Cloud), an Ojibwe, was born on the White Earth Reservation in northern Minnesota and was taken from his home and sent to boarding school for first grade. He later recalled

I, Way Quah Gishig, was six years old when my two sisters, Bishiu and Min di, accompanied me to Flandreau, South Dakota, to attend an Indian boarding school.

It was very difficult for me at first, for students at the school were not allowed to speak the language of the Indians. At that time I understood nothing else.

Neither did I like to be forced to remain with my sisters in the girls' building instead of being assigned to the quarters occupied by the boys.

I was as shy and timid as the young buck in the forest and clung very closely to my sister. But soon I learned to speak and understand a little of

Three girls wearing matching cotton-print outfits in about 1900 were probably students at an Indian boarding school.

the white man's language; and gradually the boys began coaxing me to play with them.

At first I wore my hair in two braids, Indian fashion, but at last my sisters gave in and allowed it to be cut so that I would be like the other boys.

The children didn't see their mother again for six years.

What a reunion that was! She endeavored to gather us all into her arms at once. She started talking joyously, but we couldn't understand very well what she said, for we had forgotten much of the Indian language during our six years away from home.

Eventually he started to use the name of John Rogers, which the white school called him, and to abandon the "existence of my ancestors."

But now I must return to the life that the white man had chosen for the Indian to follow—from this time on! I must read from books instead of from Nature. I must learn of the birds and the animals and the trees from books instead of daily contact with them. This was what the white man said I should do, and I could do nothing but obey.

John Rogers, 1896

Boys at the nursery school at Ponemah, on the Red Lake Reservation in Beltrami County, had some good roadwork going in about 1940. An ad for Gerber baby food is in the background. Those Gerber babies were everywhere.

Manners

Politeness, either of feeling or of manner, can never be taught by set maxims. Every-day influence, so unconsciously exerted, is all important in forming the characters of children, and in nothing more important than in their manners . . .

I recollect an anecdote, which plainly shows that politeness cannot be shuffled on at a moment's warning, like a garment long out of use. A worthy, but somewhat vulgar, woman, expected a visit from strangers of some distinction. On the spur of the occasion, she called her children together and said, "After I have dressed you up, you must sit very still, till the company comes; and then you must be sure to get up and make your bows and courtesies; and you must mind and say 'Yes, ma'am,' and 'No, ma'am,' —and 'No, sir' 'I thank you.'" The visitors arrived—and the children, seated together like "four and twenty little dogs all of a row," up rose at once bobbed their bows and courtesies and jabbered over, "Yes, ma'am—no, ma'am—yes, sir—no, sir—I thank you—There mother, now we've done it."

Lydia Maria Francis Child, 1831

A mere accident of environment about this time [in 1867], when I was fifteen but the size of a ten-year-old, put me on the truthful track.

Facing a crisis, tho a small one, something led me to stand up to the mark—an intuition, I guess. Having broken down the brick neck of neighbor

Comstock's new cistern while climbing out, I jumped the fence and went home, well scared. I didn't know just what to do. The break was an accident. Of course, I shouldn't have been in the cistern, but a boy likes above all things to "holler" in a cistern. A little after, Mr. Comstock called to [stepsister] Matie, [friend] Henry Gladding and me to ask if we knew who broke the cistern.

I said, "Yes sir, I did." Likely this was an automatic act, at any rate it was a good one, and it led me to form the habit of trying to be truthful in a crisis. Mr. Comstock said, "That's alright, no great harm done," and we children went off to our play. It might be well for folks to do as Mr. Comstock did, that is, make it easy to tell the truth. Accusation from him certainly would have made me lie, perhaps from sheer fright.

Walter Stone Pardee

IN THE MAY 25, 1889, ISSUE OF *GOOD HOUSEKEEPING*, PARENTS WERE URGED TO FEED CHILDREN UNDER FIVE YEARS OLD BEFORE ADULTS SAT FOR DINNER, OCCASIONALLY BRINGING THE CHILDREN TO THE TABLE FOR DESSERT.

Oct. 23, 1894

Please pardon me for not writing to you sooner and thanking you for the neck tie which you sent me and which was just the thing I wanted, but I thought I would wait until I got back from Duluth where we went Friday to play foot-ball and got beaten 16–10. I never had such a good time as I had up at Duluth.

Alexander Ramsey Furness to his sister Anita

This could be Easter in about 1952. Jim Shimek's pants were just out of the package; the creases still showed. The pants were big enough to grow into all summer, and the hat might have been just like dad's.

One day a young, nice-looking couple with two little boys, 6 and 8, stopped to visit with us. Somebody always was stopping. I think they got to know that if they stopped at our place we'd put them up for the night, feed them, feed their horses. My father was so big-hearted. Well, this couple's name was Heatherington. They stayed overnight with us, and when it came time to leave the next morning my folks said there wasn't any hurry. So they decided to stay a bit longer. It turned out that they stayed for *six weeks*. They said they'd been living with a bachelor who owned a farm—I don't remember why they said they left.

They were very pleasant people. They were entertaining. They could sing, tell stories, and she could sew and knew all sorts of different ways of combing hair, which was very pleasant to my older sisters. Mr. Heatherington would help with the chores. They were the sort of people you enjoyed. They made themselves agreeable. On a farm, you know, you produce food, and you never think about what it costs. I can still see that nice Heatherington lady putting the curling tongs over the lamp chimney to heat it, so she could curl our hair.

Well, later we learned that the Heatheringtons were really traveling entertainers. This was their permanent mode of life. Going from one place to the next, being companionable, helpful. But mother used to say, "Now don't be a Heatherington!" It meant, "Don't overstay your welcome."

Lillian MacGregor Shaw, about 1900

Dec. 20, 1923
Buck Hill Ranch
Savage, Minn.

Dear Aunt Josephine,

. . . I do not remember very much of you or your place the time we visited you, but one thing which seemed to leave an impression on my mind was the fact that we had either pie or cake (either was delicious) for breakfast . . .
Your loving niece,
Alice Josephine Hunt

My [St. Paul Central High] homeroom teacher, Miss Baumgarten, was a nice looking woman of small stature who had sandy-blonde hair. She mailed me a warm and caring letter in which she described how sorry she was to hear of my father's death. She described it as a major loss and assured me that over a long period of time, I would begin to understand that he would never disappear. As she phrased it, "You will always have your memories of him." She went on to offer that if I needed anything or had questions about

Mock weddings were fashionable (and cheap) entertainment for decades, and that's likely what this 1886 photo showed. Besides children's "weddings," there were manless weddings (women played the men's parts, too) and womanless weddings (even more amusing). This kids' version was more intricate than most. Notice the trains of the girls' dresses arranged daintily behind them.

anything, I could call her. I was so impressed and comforted that she cared about me. What a lovely gesture it was at such an important time of my life.

Marion Levitan Kaplan Gebner, about 1936

Music

Aug. 13. Little Mary [not yet three months old] shows a peculiar love of Harmony. When we Sing at family worship, she sometimes appears excited & commences a mellow smooth sound—significant of gratification & amusement. It would seem that she laboured to join her voice with ours.

Catherine Ely, 1836

Goodhue County farmer Lewis Johnson sent his ten-year-old son to school in Red Wing in 1879 and paid extra for private music lessons: "Paid Miss Anna Whelan for teaching Georgie Music $5.00." (Probably not for guitar lessons.)

By the time I had reached the age of 10 [in 1887], I had probably attended more country dances than any child of my age (excepting my sister, two years younger than myself) in the state of Minnesota.

My father was an old-time fiddler [near Elk River] and a very good one—so good, in fact, that he played for all the dances for miles around. Mother

This was the 1940s version of a garage band. Check out the wild drum major hat.

loved to dance, so we children were always taken along, being too young to be left at home alone. Baby sitters were unheard of.

The dances were held in the farm houses. Lumber or logs were cheap and the kitchens were large, giving ample room after the table and chairs had been pushed back against the wall for the square dance, money-musk, Virginia reel, lancers and so on.

How often do I recall my father and mother coming to the schoolhouse at 3 in the afternoon to take me home because he had to play for a dance, perhaps 10 miles away. We were hurriedly dressed, and if it was winter, on our way by 4 o'clock because travel was slow with a couple of old nags hitched to farm sleds, and we must be there not later than 7. They liked to start the fun early, and dancing usually continued on until daybreak. Then we started back home, arriving there sometimes as late as 8 in the morning—about

In about 1890, a boy played his piano lesson in the parlor, an ancestor watching from above.

time for father to begin his morning chores. It must have been very tiresome for them sitting in the cold and driving that distance after being up all night, but for my sister and I it was fun. Straw was placed on the bottom of the sled and blankets spread over it to make a bed, and with the old flat-irons heated and placed at our feet, we were as "snug as a bug in a rug" and slept as one of their old sayings went, "just like a log."

We children sat and watched the dancers until our eyes refused to stay open any longer. Then we were taken upstairs where we could lie on the bed.

I liked to sit close to my father and watch him play. I loved the old fiddle and its old tunes, and it was such fun to hear him "spell" the caller once in a while and sing out lustily these words to the "Cracovienne Quickstep": "First lady lead to the right-hand gent, Swing with the right hand, the right hand around. Back with the left and the left hand around, Lady in the center and seven hands around. Lady swing out and gent swing in, all join hands and circle again. Find your partners large and small and all promenade to your places all" . . .

Sometime during the evening, the hat was passed around and the proceeds went to the fiddler. It might be anything from a dollar up to two-fifty. Whatever the amount happened to be was always all right with father. From these meager earnings, he always kept a "wee nest egg" in the little compartment meant for strings and rosin in the old fiddle box. My first music lessons were made possible by this little surplus.

Iva Andrus Dingwall, 1880s

When Aunt Maggie and Uncle Orlando Green and my cousin Lily came, there was lots of music. Uncle Orlando would play the organ and we would all stand around him and sing—hymns, war songs and some of the popular songs of the day. I can still hear Uncle Orlando's rumbling baritone on "My Bonnie Lies Over the Ocean" and a song, very popular in those days, "Darling Clo." My favorite was one that began with the line, "White wings they never grow weary," while my mother would have tears coursing down her cheeks when the song was "Tenting Tonight." Such lovely times we had!

Blanche Stoddard Seely, 1880s

Father loved good music and was very eager that Anson and I should have a thorough musical education and be able to play something well. From the time I was a little child, Father used to take me Sunday afternoons to the Dantz concerts, which were the forerunner of the present Symphony concerts. I remember I used to get very tired and bored and fidgety toward the last half of these concerts. I started taking piano lessons when I was quite small, and I kept on taking them for years and years. Miss Mary Dillingham, who was a great friend of Mother's and Father's, was my first teacher. She used to come once or twice a week for dinner and play to Father afterwards. I remember so well her recitals . . . where all of her pupils would perform.

Charles and Sandy Turchick worked on their duet in about 1950.

What agony we went through before our turn to play! . . . No one ever saw a cuter sight than Eddie Phelps playing his first piece at about the age of 4, a little mite of a fellow in a black velvet suit with a lace collar!

I was terribly conscientious about practicing and would always put in the time I was supposed to. In the winter I would get up and practice before breakfast. Anson thought I was an awful little sap to be so good, but the result was that I stuck at it and learned to play the piano really pretty well so that it has always given me a lot of pleasure and I know gave Father a lot. Anson never got farther than "The Happy Farmer." He wouldn't take the time to practice and didn't go on, though he has a better ear than I have and fully as good an appreciation of music. Father played the violin *terribly*. As I got older, I used to accompany him on the piano. He used to simply love it, but he really did produce the most awful squeaks and sounds. It was one of our family anecdotes that even the cat put her paws over her ears when we were having one of these sessions.

Margaret Jackson Bovey, 1890s

March 28, 1911

Went to the Simfeny Orkestra. They had a harp solo and I liked that.

Glanville Smith

When I was six, I played a small violin, but after six months or so, my teacher, Miss Bendike, tactfully suggested that I should play something that didn't require tuning. A few years later, my doting father informed us that

The 1944 all-girl orchestra at St. Paul's Horace Mann School should have gotten an A in music appreciation. Who wouldn't get excited about mixing bells, cymbals, drums, a xylophone, and a tambourine?

he had ordered a flute for me and a clarinet for my brother Ted. The flute arrived first, and Ted claimed it by virtue of his seniority. A few days later came my clarinet, and my lifetime affair with woodwinds began.

Our home had a music room with a beautiful mahogany curly-legged Steinway piano, played by Rose. Bill played violin and sometime viola, Ted the flute, and I the clarinet. Our favorite music was opera overtures of which we had 30 or 40 contained in four volumes, score and parts.

The Berman orchestra played to the admiring ears of our parents, who trotted us out on any occasion to play for their friends. We played our overtures—never mind that all the parts were treble and usually on the same note . . . We reached the height of our family musical endeavors when we played the overture to *William Tell,* which had everything—resonant, slow beauty, fast tricky brilliant passages, a storm in which Rosie wiggled her left hand on the bass keys and Bill played fast runs on the G string. But best of all was the flute and English horn duet. Here Ted didn't object much to my taking the horn cues—he couldn't play the two parts simultaneously. But when the flute part had a few bars' rest, he would join in with me for a few notes of the oboe part. I never edged into his territory by playing the flute score because it was too hard for me. Ted was better on the flute than I was on my instrument . . .

We provided our parents with ineffable joy and gave the neighbors an excuse to visit their relatives on the other side of town.

Reuben Berman, 1910s

When I was 12 years old, I persuaded my mother to trade in our golden oak, upright piano for a second-hand player piano at the Foster and Waldo's Music Store on Nicollet Avenue, downtown [Minneapolis]. I don't recall the cost-balance, but I do remember taking the monthly $10 payment down to the store each month because I could then buy the latest roll. Fats Waller was my favorite QRS roll pianist.

Carl Warmington, 1919

What were young people listening to in Minnesota over the decades? We can guess, judging from vocal and instrumental music that was popular in the United States. Here's a sample:

1858, when Minnesota became a state: "Warblings at Eve," a piano solo.
1860: "Old Black Joe," by Stephen Foster. "When the Corn Is Waving, Annie Dear."
1870: "Safe in the Arms of Jesus," hymn.
1880: "Never Take the Horse Shoe from the Door." "Why Did They Dig Ma's Grave so Deep?"
1890: "Thy Beaming Eyes," a love song. "Throw Him Down, McCloskey."

A Minneapolis kinder-
garten turned into a
rhythm band, complete
with patriotic hats, in
about 1930. Music does
indeed soothe the
savage beast.

In Mankato in 1941,
a woman played for
her children. The boys
look like they got
home haircuts.

1900: "I've a Longing in My Heart for You, Louise." "Just Because She Made
      Dem Goo-Goo Eyes." "The Blue and the Gray; or, A Mother's Gift to
      Her Country."
1910: "Down by the Old Mill Stream." "Ah, Sweet Mystery of Love,"
      music by Victor Herbert. "A Banjo Song." "Call Me Up Some Rainy
      Afternoon," by Irving Berlin. "Let Me Call You Sweetheart."

Enough of that piano stuff! In 1935, these guys got to mess around with a euphonium, too big for one to hold. Notice the drop seat in the work coveralls. Convenient, eh?

1920: "All She'd Say Was 'Umh Hum,'" Ziegfeld Follies. "Daddy, You've Been a Mother to Me." "I'll Be With You in Apple Blossom Time." "Hiawatha's Melody of Love." "O Little Town of Bethlehem." "Where Do They Go When They Row, Row, Row?"

1930: "The Battle of Jericho," a Negro spiritual. "Georgia on My Mind." "Embraceable You" and "I Got Rhythm," by George and Ira Gershwin. "Them There Eyes," by Irving Berlin. "Walkin' My Baby Back Home." "What Is This Thing Called Love?" by Cole Porter.

1940: "All or Nothing at All." "The Last Time I Saw Paris," by Oscar Hammerstein and Jerome Kern. "When You Wish Upon a Star," from the film *Pinocchio.* "You Are My Sunshine."

1950: "A Bushel and a Peck," from *Guys and Dolls.* "If I Knew You Were Comin' I'd 'Ave Baked a Cake." "Goodnight, Irene." "Tennessee Waltz." "I Said My Pajamas."

1960: "Are You Lonesome To-Night?" "Camelot," by Alan Lerner and Frederick Loewe. "Cathy's Clown," the Everly Brothers. "Itsy Bitsy, Teenie Weenie, Yellow Polka-Dot Bikini." "The Twist."

Growing Up

Permanent waves, monkeying with engines, learning to drive, first jobs, first loves, first heartbreaks—they've all been part of graduating from childhood.

Fashion

BOTH BOYS AND GIRLS WORE DRESSES OR GOWNS UNTIL THEY WERE AGE SIX OR SEVEN. IN THE TIME OF THE PURITANS, A CEREMONY CALLED "BREECHING" WAS HELD TO MARK THE END OF EARLY CHILDHOOD. IT WAS THEN A BOY BEGAN TO WEAR PANTS.

Many of the Dakota women and girls wore ornaments sparingly, and exhibited good taste in selecting them. When many beads were worn, they were so arranged, by making the strings of different lengths, that they covered the throat and breast.

Their hair was combed smoothly back and braided in two braids, one behind each ear, the ends of the braids hanging down on the breast in front.

The females used little paint. The young women put a little vermilion [a brilliant red pigment] on the top of the head where the hair was parted, and, with the end of the finger, painted a small red spot on each cheek.

Samuel W. Pond, 1834

Mother got a Wheeler and Wilson sewing machine in 1863 or 1864. It was supposed to be a great help; but, as almost at once the women and girls began wearing ruffles on everything, the sewing took about as much time as it had before. We had to be stylish.

Alice Mendenhall George

YOUR CHILDREN must not be neglected. Take them to the Boson One Price Clothing Store and dress them up in style. Purmort & Steele make a specialty of children's and youth's clothing and keep a full line of all the genteel Eastern styles. How nice your boys would look dressed up in some of those handsome suits. Try it once, and you will never bother to make any more clothes for them, for two reasons—first, the clothes you make don't look half as well and your boys don't look so nice; and second, it won't cost you near as much as it does to make them yourselves. Mothers, make a note of this.

Minneapolis Tribune, June 30, 1875

We did not—indeed we could not—buy everything ready-made. I suppose people of great means could, but Mother had a sewing woman come in for ten days twice a year—and paid her, I believe, about 75 cents a day. Together, she and Mother made everything we wore: Mother's silk and broadcloth dresses and all my dresses, our underwear, chemises, corset-covers, petticoats, voluminous drawers and the underwear and shirts and handkerchiefs of fine linen for [stepfather] Ed and for my little brother. Unbleached muslin was bought by the bolt for sheets, and each year a certain number was added to the already overflowing supply in the linen closet. The sheets were first soaked with water and laid out on the grass to bleach, with both sun and rain beating down on them. Pillow slips, kitchen towels, bath towels—all those things were made at home. Damask table cloths and napkins were hand-hemmed; Grandma Hall did most of those.

Blanche Stoddard Seely, 1880s

Mother went off on a week's visit. Papa didn't think to have us save our white dresses for the next Sunday. We played about happily all week, but I

Velvet and frills and bows—this extravagant outfit in about 1895 was called a Lord Fauntleroy suit. The poor fellow's hair was curled and his shoes were shined to a gloss to complete the ensemble.

Hans Carl Schmidt modeled his first trousers in about 1903. Babies and toddlers—boys as well as girls—wore dresses, usually until they were potty trained, making diaper changing a lot easier for moms. Both parents and babies benefited when safety pins began to replace straight pins on diapers in the late 1800s.

remember the look of consternation when we looked at ourselves and each other in our soiled dresses.

Jo Lutz Rollins, 1890s

In those days, boys wore short pants until they were 12 to 14 years old. Mother thought George was old enough to have long pants. There was a big fire sale advertised in the paper, so on Saturday morning Mother gave me $6, and George, Carl and I went to town to get George a suit. We walked all the way, about five miles. The fire sale suits were $5. We looked at the suit, and it fit George fine, but he didn't know if that was the suit he wanted. The salesman was getting disgusted with us. We argued and said to George, "Either take the suit or say no." Carl and I were anxious to get to a movie. In those days it was just five cents and you could go and sit all day if you wanted to. George finally bought the suit, black with white stripes. We went over to the Plymouth Building in Minneapolis (that's where we generally bought a suit) and here he could have gotten a blue serge suit for the same price. So we went back with the striped suit, but they would not take it back. We went to the movie and stayed a long time. Then we walked home. George couldn't forget the nice serge suit he could have got for $5, so he kept complaining that we had talked him into buying a no-good suit. He kept it up and kept it up. When we got to the bridge, Carl was so fed up with his complaining that he said, "If you don't shut up, I'll throw you over the bridge." The suit turned out to be a terrible poor one. After George wore it several times, the white faded out in spots.

Lena L. Borchardt, about 1900

This father and son, photographed in Albert Lea, wore matching styles of formal outerwear in about 1898. Often in the past, children were dressed as miniature versions of adults. We hope the boy grew into the coat. Meanwhile, he doesn't seem to mind its size.

Now when the timber was cut, the new growth that followed was prime deer food. All the neighbors shot deer. The red hides couldn't be sold, so they brought them to me and I tanned them, keeping one out of three. I doused them in the creek until the hair could be scrubbed off, then tanned and oiled the hides. There was one awful stink where that old hair collected. Finally I had enough hide for a jacket, vest and britches. The pants had a heavy charge of buckshot in the seat and were never any good, but the jacket was used for many years and never wore out.

Robert C. Shaw, early 1900s

Dad usually cut my hair on a Saturday so that I would look sharp for Sunday School. He was a good [amateur] barber and did as fine a job as any pro . . . I recall with special poignancy that Dad had a healthy masculine aroma about him—something I have never before mentioned to anyone. I became aware of this when my father cut my hair. He wore the usual shirt and pants which were his powerhouse uniform [worn when he operated the Twin City Rapid Transit Company's power substation on Lowry Avenue and Third Street in north Minneapolis]. Perhaps the smell of his body and the atmosphere of the substation mingled to make the scent that was distinctly his. I liked it and remember it with acute nostalgia. No barber has smelled so good in all the years since then.

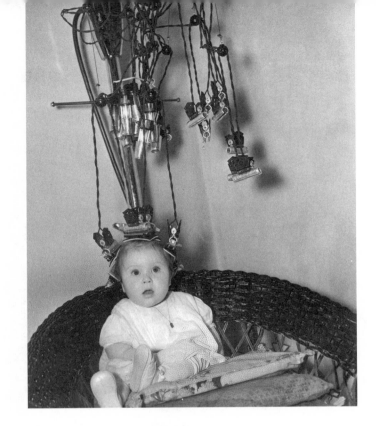

Poor baby: she was getting a permanent wave at a beauty shop in about 1938. How did they get the little one to sit still in that contraption? Girls and women said their scalps frequently were burned by the machines. Ah, for beauty!

Dad always finished the job like an expert as he rubbed his own blend of petroleum jelly and bay rum into my hair. Then he carefully parted and combed my hair before bringing out a wooden-framed, rectangular mirror so I could inspect his work. After I got down from the chair, which was his wooden-armed office swiveler with a board across the arms, there was always a treat. Often it was a horehound lozenge or a piece of licorice. To this day they are among my favorite candies.

Melvin Lynn Frank, 1910s

Getting a perm in those days was quite a procedure and sometimes risky. The permanent wave machines were a contraption, to say the least. The thing loomed over one's head like an octopus with many rope-like arms. At the end of every "arm" was a metal clamp which was attached to each perm rod, so there a person sat with this monster affixed to her scalp. Mom and I sometimes went to a beauty school in St. Paul where they offered their services at a low cost. One time, my mother went there to get a curly do and ended up with a bad burn on her neck. The hot steam from the perm machine had scalded her. She screamed out and the gals all came running to attend to her. They felt so bad and fussed over her, applying salve to her tender, pink skin.

To get our hair to keep a nice finger wave, we went to the grain elevator and bought a handful of flax seed for a nickel, carrying it home in a little paper bag. We boiled the tiny seeds in water until a thick, slimy mixture was

By the 1930s, sailor suits were hot even for swaggering little guys. The emblem on his cap says NORGE, Norwegian for "Norway." Maybe Papa was a sailor in the Norwegian Navy. Blue historically was the prevalent color for military and school uniforms and for servants' clothing because blue dye was the cheapest. (Centuries earlier, it was believed that evil spirits were allergic to the color blue. Boys were considered more important than girls, so blue was reserved for them.)

created. We put the homemade setting gel in our hair, placing in the waves just so with fingers, then sat out in the sunshine to dry.

Mary Gilson Ferguson, late 1920s

Before the natural look became acceptable (to blacks as well as to whites), getting your hair done was a lengthy process, and—if you didn't keep your head still—a painful one. I hated it, and I was always glad when I could be first, so I wouldn't have to think about it all day. Miss Jackson was fast and efficient, but she was far from gentle.

First she combed the kinks out of my hair with the large straightening comb. Then she used the hot pullers (tongs with ball ends flattened on the insides) to straighten small clumps of hair. The small heated straightening comb was used on the short hair around the edges of the hairline, sometimes producing burns. You could also be burned if the curling iron got caught in the little curls; feeling the heat, you might pull away and bring the hot iron onto your head.

But beauty is in the eye of the beholder, and we all thought we looked better after we had gone through this painful and sometimes disfiguring exercise at least twice a month. (Rain, humidity, or sweat could undo the job in less than an hour.) Someone always remarked about how *everyone*

Philip Wilson, in short pants, lisle stockings, and curls, stood at his back porch in Stillwater in about 1903. Little boys didn't wear long pants until they were between eight and twelve years old.

could understand why Madame C. J. Walker, who invented and marketed the lotions and straightening combs we used, was the first black millionaire in this country.

Evelyn Fairbanks, 1930s

Mom sewed everything. I think the only store-bought dress that I had before was when I made my First Communion. It was white, in sort of an organdy, and it had blue dots on it, heaven forbid. When I made the First Communion, the nuns were very upset, because it wasn't pure white. When there was 40 hours devotion at church, and all the second-grade girls at that time would be marching in their white dresses, I couldn't because I had the blue dots on my dress.

Marietta Neumann, mid-1930s

Raymond, left, and Eva Munson wore their winter coats in about 1900. Yes, truly, that's Raymond on the left. He wasn't the only boy dressed that way. Call it high fashion.

Hand in the pocket of his overalls, this little guy brimmed with confidence in about 1895. A Minneapolis commercial photographer took the shot.

Fashion plates in St. Paul in 1929: Jack, Bob, and Ralph Jones. Two of the boys wore knickers, one shorts.

Inventions

Charlotte Ouisconsin Clark was only a few weeks old in 1819 when her parents came to the region to help establish the first military post, later called Fort Snelling. When she was five years old, she saw the arrival of the first steamboat. Much later, in 1888, the then Charlotte Van Cleve wrote about her excitement.

Perhaps the most distinct of my early remembrances is the arrival of the first steamboat. It had been talked of and expected for a long time; it is hard to realize in this age of rapid traveling how deeply interested and excited every one felt in anticipation of what was then a great event. It was to bring us into more direct and easy communication with the world; and small wonder that the prospect of being at the head of steamboat navigation should have caused excitement and rejoicing to those who had been receiving their mails at intervals of *months* instead of *hours.* To me, of course, child that I was, it only meant a sight never before witnessed, a something heard of, and seen in pictures [paintings or sketches; this was decades before photography], but never realized. But even we children felt in listening to our elders that something great was about to happen.

At last, one bright summer morning, while amusing myself on the piazza in the rear of the officers' quarters, there came a sound new and very strange! All listened a moment in awe and gratitude, and then broke out from many voices, "The steamboat is coming! The steamboat is coming!" And look! There is the smoke curling gracefully through the trees; hark! To the puffing of the steam, startling the echoes from a sleep; now she rounds the point and comes into full view. I stand on tiptoe, but cannot see all I long to, till Lieutenant David Hunter, my special favorite, catches me up and holds me on the balustrade; and now I clap my hands, and almost cry with delight, for there she is, just landing, in all her pride and beauty, as if she *felt* herself the Pioneer Steamboat and knew she would become historic.

Out camping, little Muriel Prindle of Duluth and a woman—probably her mother, Mina—were wrapped in mosquito netting. The day in about 1900 must have been too buggy to lounge in that nice hammock (at left).

Imagine: Praise for screens on windows to keep out bugs!

I recall nothing of fly screens for house openings in the New England of my youth . . . Wire screens were not made, so far as I know . . . I guess that sometime the sixties [1860s] someone thot of mosquito netting, so called, a flimsy cotton fabric that might last [only] a summer or so and not keep insects away either. This was apt to be put over a bed, or perhaps a settler in the primitive forest of the west might put one over his head. When I got to Minnesota in 1866, a farmer who had taken up a forest land claim told me that he, for instance in carrying pails of water, would have his hands and neck mostly black with mosquitoes. He might or might not take time to brush them off. Never mind such trifles, he thot; but if he only had known it, he was lucky in that the mosquitoes were of the harmless kind. That was one of the good things about Minnesota, near Minneapolis at least . . .

About this time, folks in St. Anthony, Minn., thot they had solved the problem when they devised the cloth netting to go over the bed, the netting lying on a light frame; but the screening of windows and doors was too much of a venture. The bed screen was a nuisance, especially with two people in a bed, for one or the other would leave a mosquito hole, or make one as the night wore on; while the insects had a way of finding the smallest passable hole.

But now came the person with the bright idea: "Why not put some cloth netting on an open window?" he said, and so he did. But there would be only one to a room and that over one half of the window. To cover one half of all the windows and all the doors would have been reckless waste, and I guess it would have been, too, for the netting was ready to break at the first touch.

By and by, even those of us who were some hardened to mosquito bites, got the notion of screens and their use; and after that, screens we must have. Flies still were taken as a matter of course . . . I would say that not until the last ten years [the 1910s] have flies been frowned upon. Very neat housekeepers and some advanced thinkers barred flies, especially in the front parlor that was kept dark and shut up mostly; but folks commonly had flies aplenty in the house . . . Likely it was along in the late seventies in Minneapolis that wire fly screens were applied to all house openings.

Walter Stone Pardee

When Marion Ramsey was ten years old, a professor brought a hot-air balloon to St. Paul. Most people declined a ride, but the gutsy Ramseys volunteered.

The weather proving fair, Professor Steiner made about twenty army ascensions yesterday afternoon. He was unable to take up more than one passenger on each ascension, owing to a deficiency in the supply of gas. It required 41,000 cubic feet to inflate the balloon, and the Gas Company was unable to supply more than 36,000 feet . . .

One of the richest incidents of the day was the attempt of [U.S.] Senator Ramsey to pay a visit to the realms of space. He got into the balloon and rose in the air about thirty feet, but the specific gravity of the Senator was so great [he was a hefty guy at five feet eight and more than 220 pounds] that all the gas the balloon held was insufficient to elevate him above the roofs of the houses, and he had to be deposited on terra firma, evidently much disappointed, and vowing that he would undergo a course of vegetarian training to enable him at some future opportunity, to take the position of champion of the light weights.

Boys lined up with their homemade wooden train in the Ellestad backyard of Lanesboro in about 1908. They wore "visiting clothes," a step or two up from play clothes.

But the Ramsey blood was bound to show itself, and Miss Marion Ramsey, a young lady of ten years, made the ascent on her own account, and said, when she came down, that her only regret was that she could not stay up long enough.

St. Paul Pioneer Press, August 20, 1863

Isaac Haycraft was about five years old in 1870 when he saw his first train, and a scary sight it was.

The talk of the new railroad was fast becoming the main topic of conversation. Finally the word was passed around that, on a certain day and at a certain hour, the first train to travel on the new railroad was to pass through Madelia. It seemed that every man, woman and child for miles around made it a point to be on hand at the depot to witness the event. Some of the older boys who had seen an engine hauling a train told us smaller boys the most horrifying tales about this snorting puffing monster. We had a bad case of the jitters before it ever came in sight and when it actually did come, it was just a little too much for a small boy to face and stand his ground. I admit I took to my heels and soon placed a safe distance between myself and that terrible bell-ringing, whistle-blowing contraption. I stuck pretty close to my parents until that awful outfit moved on to the next town.

*　　*　　*

Several warriors had observed from a distance one of the first trains on the Northern Pacific, and had gained an exaggerated impression of the wonders of the pale-face. They had seen it go over a bridge that spanned a deep ravine, and it seemed to them that it jumped from one bank to the other. I confess that the story almost quenched my ardor and bravery.

Two or three young men were talking together about this fearful invention.

"However," said one, "I understand that this fire-boat-walks-on-mountains cannot move except on the track made for it."

Although a boy is not expected to join in the conversation of his elders, I ventured to ask: "Then it cannot chase us into any rough country?"

"No, it cannot do that," was the reply, which I heard with a great deal of relief.

Charles Eastman, 1870s

[Minneapolis] held a wonderful exposition, and a family friend who had something to do with the selection of pictures and sculptures to be exhibited offered me a position on the grounds, demonstrating Mr. Edison's talking machine. It was the first time it had been shown in Minneapolis.

Into one of the smaller art rooms had been built a row of five or six little rooms with a door at each end of each room. Inside were six ordinary chairs and a table on which rested the little black box—the talking machine—and six sets of ear-phones. At one side of one of these tables I sat, handing each person who came in an ear-phone and, when six had assembled, turning on the machine. It was wonderful! People were so thrilled, as I was, and the booth was always filled. They seemed never to tire of the miracle of it, for they would go out one door, walk around to the end of the line and come back in. It was a happy time for me, for I loved meeting so many different people. I remember one group, a father and mother and a son of perhaps 15. They came back again and again, and finally the woman said, "Just think, John. You'll be able to record all your sermons!" The son groaned, and I tried not to laugh.

And oh, it was such a thin little voice that came out of the black box, but every word was distinct and clear. It was truly the beginning of a new world.

Blanche Stoddard Seely, 1880s

Way back in the 1890s, two schoolboys in Northfield built some of America's first gasoline motor-driven vehicles. (Henry Ford produced his first Model T in 1908.) In a reminiscence written in the 1930s, Lincoln Fey described how he

Hitting the road: brothers Lincoln and Frank Fey of Northfield posed with the second car they built, in 1898.

constructed a very small, single-engine, three-wheel vehicle in 1895–97, with help from his brother, Frank.

As I finished different parts, I brought them home and assembled the tricycle in our barn. Along toward spring of 1896 the machine was complete, with the exception of levers to control the rig, in addition to the steering lever. Over-anxious to try the machine, my brother and I pushed it out in the street. The engine was started. (The only means available to stop it was to pull a wire off the igniter.) I got into the seat. The clutch cone was chucked in by my brother with a stick, and away I went down the street. On making the first turn, I nearly upset, and it was evident that the steering gear was very sensitive. The tricycle gained speed in every block and I was due for a smash-up, as farther down the street I would have to go down hill. I decided to try to make the turn at the next crossing. Swinging gradually over to one side of the street, I attempted to make the turn, but to keep from upsetting, headed the tricycle up over the sidewalk and into a snowbank. My brother had been following up on the run and came up all out of breath and aglow with excitement. This was one of the most thrilling moments of our lives. The vehicle was pulled out of the snowbank and some time was spent in trying to start the engine, but with no success. So we pushed the contrivance back to the barn . . .

Many times in those days I ventured the prediction to my parents that we would see the time when horse-drawn vehicles would become a thing of the past. But dad, being a lover of horses, couldn't see it that way and cautioned us continually to leave anything that used gasoline alone or we would be blown up. Mother, however, was different and, true to a mother's tradition, steadfastly offered encouragement all along.

The Fey boys sold the tricycle and built a larger four-wheel "horseless carriage" in 1897–98, a single-cylinder four-passenger automobile in 1901–2, and a four-passenger automobile with an air-cooled, four-cylinder engine in 1904–5. They sold each one to finance construction of the next.

I went to stay overnight with Imogene Latz to some friends of hers in Mankato. They had indoor plumbing. I had to go to the bathroom in the night, and when I pulled the string, the toilet kept on running. I thought I'd broken it and worried for years about it.

Jo Lutz Rollins, 1910s

Prior to the purchase of a spark coil for use in our wireless station, we had been involved in various ways with induction coils which provided relatively weak electric shocks. One such device had been made by father, and it became a part of our stock of apparatus. I remember it quite distinctly as my brother, while visiting a friend at his farm home, had used it, in collaboration with his friend, to contrive a "hot" seat in the outhouse, preparatory to its

Kids tried out the seat of their toy airplane in the 900 block of East Minnehaha Street, St. Paul, in about 1930. Somebody spin the propeller, please.

With concentration galore, this child (boy? girl?) tried a hand at the wheel in about 1935. We presume the car was not running.

anticipated occupancy by the hired man. Although I was neither a witness to, nor an accomplice in, that happening, I was later told that the mission was accomplished, with some objections from the hired man.

Gerhard A. Ellestad, about 1913

Although automobiles were long in existence, we boys would run from the house to see a car drive by—the first I remember was a Brush roadster—but what really roused every child on [north Minneapolis's] Elwood Avenue was the alarm bell of Number 16 Fire Engine from the station two blocks away on Knox and Fifth. The engine was a steam pumper pulled by three horses. The galloping horses—sparks flying from their iron shoes—the engine with its vertical boiler, all gleaming and polished, red and silver, and the fire box trailing red ashes are permanent memories for those of us who saw this romantic 19th-century anachronism. Children still gawk at fire engines, of course, but no amount of gasoline-driven horsepower can equal the thrilling sight of three horses tearing along, pulling that lovely mechanism behind!

Reuben Berman, 1910s

We began to hear stories about a new invention that could transmit sound from distant places without the use of wires like the telephone.

My first introduction to this was in 1927 at a neighbor's when I was astonished to hear voices and music coming out of a pair of headphones. This marvelous new object was known as a radio. I decided that I had to have one of these gadgets too, but my parents were less than enthusiastic. My mother said that we would have to string a wire to the broadcasting

Kids listened to the radio at Sheltering Arms, a Minneapolis social-service agency, in 1929. Voices from a box: incredible.

tower which was seven miles away, and my father couldn't believe that a real human voice could come out of a pair of earphones. They had never had such contraptions in Dvinsk [Russia, then Latvia] so how could it be real? However, I persisted and one day when my cousin, Bud Katz, was visiting from Minneapolis, he told me that not only was it possible for me to have a radio but that we could build one ourselves.

The earliest radios were crystal sets, and it took very few parts to build one. The first thing one needed was a crystal of galena, hence the term crystal set. Then a needle-like probe was mounted on a little swing fashioned from a piece of tin. Next, copper wire was wound around a cylindrical oatmeal box with one end of the wire connected to a receptacle in which the galena crystal was situated. The other end of the wire was connected to an aerial which was a 100-foot-long copper wire that went out of the window and to the roof of the barn. Finally, a ground wire ran from the set to an iron rod driven into the earth outside the window where the radio was positioned. All that was needed now was one or two sets of headphones, which we obtained from Sears Roebuck for $1.50 each.

A whole new world opened up to us . . . We listened to the farm market reports, although we didn't understand anything about them. There were news reports and musical recitals, choirs, . . . "Silent Cal" Coolidge broadcasting a speech to the nation . . . The radio set was a miracle to us.

Morris Freedland, mid-1920s

Hey, kids, don't try this
at home! Wasn't that
a can of gasoline? Ron
Keagle was the star of this
advertising postcard for
Toro Power Mower
in about 1938. Maybe
the company didn't have
a legal department
back then.

Feeding the chickens
was this child's task in
about 1900.

Jobs

My parents were on the Buckmore farm [near modern-day University Avenue and Highway 280]. Father, played out by overwork in his business, and [step]mother Fannie having consumption [tuberculosis], turned at last from city life to farm experience in the hope of getting well. In April 1866, I was nearing 14 and undersized, and found myself on the Buckmore farm where most were sick, excepting sister Mary and me. [Other families lived in the house too.]

Was ever a boy hungry clear to his toes so put upon? I was the only eater of quantity there was in the family, and why not? I was doing a man's work every day on the farm . . . During that summer, I began to think life wasn't worth living, almost, seeing that it was slow death to eat anything that tasted good. But carrying bushels of corn all day, two or three rods from bin to corncrib, or working at haying in the hot sun, or doing the usual chorework on a farm, gave such an appetite that I ate everything set before me—no questions asked . . .

Older folks, when well, always were busy, and the idea was to train a child to be busy. There were no games and no play of any kind, save perhaps a bit by [friend] Henry Gladding and me, in the snow likely or in the barn, tho sometimes after the wood was cut I was allowed to go skating on Johnson's pond.

Walter Stone Pardee, 1866

W. E. B. DuBois, a black educator and writer who led the modern American movement for full equality of blacks, was a waiter at a resort hotel on Lake Minnetonka in 1888. He had recently graduated from Fisk University. Some of his black colleagues at the hotel were teenagers. DuBois didn't name the hotel, but his description matches James J. Hill's gigantic Hotel Lafayette, with its 1,200-foot Queen Anne–style veranda. In his autobiography, he included this chilling description of the young people working there.

I entered that broad and blatant hotel at Lake Minnetonka with distinct foreboding. The flamboyant architecture, the great verandas, rich furniture and richer dresses awed us mightily. The long loft reserved for us, with its clean little cots was reassuring; the work was not difficult—but the meals! There were no meals. At first, before the guests ate, a dirty table in the kitchen was hastily strewn with uneatable scraps. We novices were the only ones who came to eat, while the guests' dining room, with its savor and sights, set our appetites on edge! After a while even the pretense of meals for us was dropped. We were sure we were going to starve when Dug, one of us, made a starting discovery; the waiters stole their food and they stole the best. We gulped and hesitated. Then we stole, too (or, at least, they stole and

I shared) and we all fattened, for the dainties were marvelous. You slipped a bit here and hid it there; you cut off extra portions and gave false orders; you dashed off into darkness and hid in corners and ate and ate! It was nasty business. I hated it. I was too cowardly to steal much myself, and not coward enough to refuse what others stole.

Our work was easy, but insipid. We stood about and watched overdressed people gorge. For the most part we were treated like furniture and were supposed to act the wooden part. I watched the waiters even more than the guests. I saw that it paid to amuse and to cringe. One particular black man set me crazy. He was intelligent and deft, but one day I caught sight of his face as he served a crowd of men; he was playing the clown—crouching, grinning, assuming a broad dialect when he usually spoke good English— ah! It was a heart-breaking sight, and he made more money than any waiter in the dining-room.

I did not mind the actual work or the kind of work, but it was the dishonesty and deception, the flattery and cajolery, the unnatural assumption that worker and diner had no common humanity. It was uncanny. It was inherently and fundamentally wrong. I stood staring and thinking, while the other boys hustled about. Then I noticed one fat hog, feeding at a heavily gilded trough, who could not find his waiter. He beckoned me. It was not his voice, for his mouth was too full. It was his way, his air, his assumption. Thus Caesar ordered his legionnaires or Cleopatra her slaves. Dogs recognized the gesture. I did not. He may be beckoning yet for all I know, for something froze within me. I did not look his way again. Then and there I disowned menial service for me and my people.

*   *   *

No one in town [Turtle River] had refrigeration, and only the stores and saloons had ice boxes to keep things cold. Milk was delivered each day by persons that had cows, and every one either sold or bought milk . . .

We bought a cow and then we had to sell milk and deliver it each morning and evening. This was quite a chore, as in the wintertime it was dark by the time the cow was milked and we then had to take a lantern and deliver the milk in pails to the customers. We tried to have only a few of the customers near home with evening deliveries and then we would have to get up early and deliver all the rest before going to school. My mother, having been raised on a farm, loved cows and did the milking, but it was my job to bring the cow in from pasture morning and night for milking. Some mornings I would have to walk through wet grass to the farthest corner of the pasture to find our cow. In the winter time there was cleaning of the barn and bringing in hay and water. Each morning and night in the winter, I had to walk the cow to the lake, cut a hole in the ice and give her water, or carry water by pail about a block to her. Most of the time I took her to the lake and on cold

A boy drove a goat-pulled wagon loaded with straw in about 1910. See the telephone lines in the background? Progress.

mornings with the wind and snow blowing, it made you wonder why people had to have cows and drink milk. My mother would have the cow milked and the milk put up in five-pound syrup pails ready for delivery by the time I was out of bed in the wintertime and start me off to deliver the milk on my way to school. I did not love this job and did considerable complaining, but usually got the milk delivered each morning and still got to school on time. However, I was very glad when the Blakley family moved into the house next to ours and had several cows and took over most of our milk customers.

J. C. "Buzz" Ryan, 1910s

Val Bjornson gave his four small children a ride on a tractor in 1954.

We enjoyed a life [in Lanesboro] that was serene and relatively simple, with no one suffering from the lack of food, clothing or shelter. While the necessities of life were ample, spending money for the kids did not fall like manna from heaven. I doubt if we had even heard of such a thing as the parental weekly allowance and, if we had, it would have taxed our credulity. So we had to hustle to earn a few pennies and nickels which we could spend as we wished—whether it be for fire crackers, candy, fish hooks, marbles or a piece of pie at the lunch counter . . .

If a kid had good luck fishing, he might peddle fresh fish from door to door. When the bass season opened on May 29th, there was a demand for minnows and soft-shell crabs for use as bait . . .

We also engaged, for profit, in an operation which today would be called recycling. The village had five saloons, and by scouting along the half-dozen roads that entered the village, one could pick up empty beer bottles and whiskey flasks. Since our parents frowned on this procedure, it had to be carried on in a clandestine manner with the bottles carried in a sack or covered basket. One saloon had a rear door which was somewhat obscured so that we could approach it from the alley without being too much in the view of the public. We brought our bottles to this door, rapped timidly to announce our presence, turned over our stuff and collected from two to four cents per bottle . . .

One or two of the kids trapped muskrats and, as I remember, received about fifty cents per pelt. I sold surplus vegetables from our garden with my main crop being late cabbage, which was handled through the local stores . . . When the local canning factory was packing sweet corn, there were sometimes a few jobs available for the kids. Almost always, a kid could join the folks who were husking corn by hand. Removing the silk and breaking off the stem at the butt of the ear were not quick and easy tasks, but they had to be done. The foreman constantly reminded the kids that corn silk was OK for pigs and cows but not for humans. The compensation for producing a heaping bushel basket of husked ears was three cents, so the kids were not exactly enthused by that job. A kid might engage in husking sporadically until he had filled ten or twelve baskets and then quit and collect his money.

Gerhard A. Ellestad, 1910s

I have not gotten along with some writers who tried to work with me before because they always wanted to turn my story into something amazing to fit their preconceptions, like we had to overcome prejudice every day. The truth is, growing up, we were a normal family, a hardworking bunch, and we were treated like a normal family. No one these days wants to believe a black family could ever be ordinary. I told someone who wanted me to do [a] book, that's what it's all about—that you don't have to be Superman or

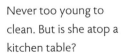

Never too young to clean. But is she atop a kitchen table?

The Garcia family worked in the sugar beet fields near New Ulm in about 1940.

Superwoman to accomplish things. You can be a regular person just like everyone else.

When I talk about normalcy, it was like the Lundquists, our neighbors when we were growing up. They went through the same shenanigans about blessing their family, told their kids to be there at the dinner table, paid attention to their kids, their cleanliness. We were normal that way.

The other thing that writers wanted to do is pigeonhole me as something they wanted me to be—black activist this, feminist that. The truth is, a lot of how I think of myself comes from the farm, a farm gal from [Lakeville and Pine County] Minnesota. One thing you need to know about my background is, it's almost all on the farm. Even people who know me tend to forget that because I've been in the city so long.

Nellie Stone Johnson, 1910s

When I was six or seven years old [on the Canadian border], my [Ojibwe] grandma had a little rabbit snare line for me in back of the house. That was my job in the morning. I would get up first thing and go lift the snares. I'd bring home a rabbit and that would be our breakfast that day, shared by all.

Grandma would clean it and make a soup and that would be breakfast. It was usually about ten or eleven o'clock when we got the rabbit cleaned and cooked. We always ate just two meals; about ten or ten-thirty in the morning, and four in the afternoon.

Betty Powell Skoog, 1930s

Teens

Alpheus Beede Stickney moved from Maine to Minnesota as a young lawyer in 1861, "in poor health and poor in purse." He became wealthy by building and running railroads. The father of eight children, he wrote letters that show him adept at child psychology.

St. Paul, Minn.
Feb. 20, 1885

My dear Son [Sam, a nineteen-year-old student at the Massachusetts Institute of Technology],

Yours of the 15th received.

I have no means of knowing whether you spend more money than

A nattily attired teenage boy had his studio portrait made in about 1900.

necessary or not. I have every confidence in you, and for that reason I do not think you do.

I know, my dear son, that you would not use money for any dishonorable or useless purpose, and beyond that I do not care to enquire. It is one of the most useful branches of education to understand how to make money, buy most of the comforts of life and also to learn how to make life comfortable with the smallest possible expense. I am entirely satisfied with you, and it is one of the greatest pleasures of my life to know that my dear children are growing up to be useful and honorable members of society and useful citizens of the world.

This, I have the fullest confidence, will be your aim and honest endeavor, and this, as I have already said, gives me very great pleasure. I will send you some more money in a day or two.

All well at home, weather very cold, but pleasant.

Very truly yours,

A. B. Stickney

In 1916, Charles Lindbergh spent the spring driving his father on a campaign trip. He was fourteen. The elder Lindbergh, Charles Sr., was running for U.S. Congress. Even then, the younger Lindbergh worried about running out of gas, this time in their Saxon Six automobile. Later, his fuel concerns were for transatlantic flight. He kept meticulous notes in a tiny diary.

Monday, April 24

We got into Minneapolis at 7:50 AM and met Raymond at the station. We took breakfast across from the station and then took the street car for the West Hotel where I am to stay tonight. From there we walked to the Saxon place where we met Farrow and a garage man. We purchased some supplies, an outer tire, extra, etc., and then the man took Farrow to the station and took me to a side street and taught me to run the car. The Saxon, he said, was the best car he ever rode in.

April 26

I got up at 6 this morning. Father went to Melrose by train as the roads are very bad. I took the car to the Saxon Agency here and they replaced a valve, which was leaking gas, from one of their own cars for 75 cents.

May 16

We started for Duluth about noon and followed the trail. The roads are the worst I have ever been over, barring none, and they keep on getting worse. We stopped over night at Rush City and I went over the car a little.

May 17

Today we went on. It rained on and off all day and we stopped over night at Sandstone where we went to the queries [quarries].

May 18

We started again this morning, and it rained a little. The machine is full of dirt and clay. We struck a rock today and knocked the top of it off. It wasn't high enough to hit the car but it was soft ground and we sank down in it. We got some dirt in the cogs and were delayed some time before I got it out. When we were about 16 miles from Duluth, the gas got low and we didn't know if we had enough to last us or not and there were no side [gas] stations before West Duluth so when we got to the top of one of the many hills which surround Duluth we would turn off the gas and let the machine coast down. This went all right until we got to the top of the highest hill passing over West Duluth and we started to coast down but the hill got steeper and steeper and as it curved around a lot, we could not see the end of it. Then I put on breaks that stopped the progress until they got loose and the hill got steeper. We were going so fast that the gear wouldn't go in and then in front of us down the steepest part of the hill was the railroad tracks and a freighter in the middle. The gate was down and there was no way to stop. A slight rise in the ground (about 50 ft. from the tracks) slowed us down a little but the gate was right in front of us. We were going from 15 to 20 miles per [hour] and if we went through the gate we might hit the train beyond. There was a slight opening about the width of the car between the gate and the track and full of deep clay. I turned into that and as there was nothing could go through it, we stopped in about ten feet. Nothing was hurt but there was no getting out of that hole so we got a grocery team, but it, ten or so men and the power of the car couldn't get us out. Then the yard master came along and offered us a tow out with a locomotive that was near by. When it got on the cable it just lifted the car right out and we went on.

William M. Cummings was expelled from several St. Paul schools and completed the largest part of high school at the University of Minnesota Farm School and Mechanic Arts High School, but did not graduate. His interests in 1933 as a teen ran to movies, hopping trucks and freight trains, bird watching, raising rabbits, peddling newspapers at the state fair, and throwing parties with his friends. He was fifteen when he fell in love with Alice D.

Sat. January 14 [1933]. I have fallen in love with Alice D. who is 2 yrs. younger than I am. It was 6 degrees below this morning. Went downtown alone & saw William Haines in "Fast Life" at the Lyceum & "Blonde Captive" at the

Somebody took a snapshot of these teens on a car on Hopkins Street, St. Paul, in 1937. The scene looks like the Upper Swede Hollow neighborhood of St. Paul.

R.K.O. President. Got home at 4:00 o'clock & played around the ice until supper.

Thurs. January 19. Got up at 7:15. Aunt Lola was here. Ratted [skipped] school & saw Jensen downtown & met another kid. Went to the R.K.O. Orpheum & saw Sherlock Holmes in "The Sign of the Four." Got a present for Alice. Haven't seen her since Mon. Listened to the radio & went & bought a jigsaw puzzle.

Fri January 20. Got caught for ratting yesterday & last week. I didn't even get scolded by Edwards, he just laughed. Had good luck in getting rides home. Put a hard jigsaw puzzle together. Went skating after supper. I hoped Alice is there. She was there. I didn't skate with her. She can't go with me so I guess it's all off.

Mon. January 23. My rabbit was sick this morning. Didn't get to school until nine o'clock. Ratted school at 12:50 P.M. & went to dentist at the University. Got a snake & took it to scout meeting.

Tues January 24. Ratted school & went sliding . . .

Wed. January 25. Went [to] 12 shows this year. An average of one show every other day . . .

February 2. Went to school today. Heard a good story in civics about homesteading. Didn't do much after school. Went down town & tried to sneak into the shows but didn't succeed. Hopped a cattle truck home & tried to sneak into the Hamline [Theater].

February 3. Went to school today. Got excused at 1:35. There is a good-looking nurse who excuses me easy. Went to the library & read. Snuck into the Hamline & saw Edward Robinson in "Tiger Shark." It was the eighteenth show I saw this year. They were nearly all good shows.

Thurs. February 9. Went to the nurses room today because Donald Wilms sat on my head. He weighs 235 lbs . . .

Sun. July 30. Read all the papers. Ate a swell dinner. Aunt Lola and Uncle came up. Went to St. Clair Theater & saw "The Eagle & The Hawk." Took Rhoda Ann Bennett & another girl. They ain't bad looking. They live in North Dakota . . .

Weds., August 2 [at my uncle's farm near Red Wing]. It rained all day. Cleaned out the calves pens. Hauled manure to the East pasture. The "honey bus" got broken. Filled the calves pens over again. Put fresh straw in them. Aunt Lola read to us. Went to bed early.

Sun. August 13. Glen and I went to see a ball game at Hendricks. Went 70 miles an hour in second [gear]. Not bad for a new V8 Ford.

Mon. August 14. Got tired of working so cheaply [on the farm] so I hopped a passenger train home. I got real dirty but it was a lot of fun. It took an hour to go 48 miles. Hopped a cattle truck home from Robert Street bridge.

Sat. August 19. Went to Monkeys [Montgomery Wards] & bought some new pants. I needed them as all my clothes are down at Red Wing.

Tues. September 12. Started to Mechanic Arts High School. It isn't bad for a school. Saw a lot of kids I knew at Wilson, Murray and Sanford [schools].

Weds., September 13. Took some books back & drew pictures & listened to the radio. The programs are getting good again. Mother & Daddy had a fight at midnight.

Thurs. September 28. Went to school. Had an assembly. Daddy has gone to live with Grandpa Cummings. Went to Newell Park with Mother & the girls for supper. Had a swell time. Went to bed real early.

Fri. September 29. Went to school. Came home & Mother had tried to kill herself. Went to a football game between Mechanics and Cretin. We won, 14 to 6. Ate at Aunt Alice's. Mother came home about 8:30 P.M. I was the only one who knew it.

Sat. September 30. Got up at 4:00 A.M. Went down to the Burlington freight yards & hopped a freight to LaCrosse. It started at 8:30 A.M. & got there at 12:30 P.M. Went to Margie's house. She had her hair cut short. She sure is pretty. Hopped a passenger [train] home. Made it in two hours.

Sun. October 1. Went to Red Wing. Mother is going to stay there for a few days. Uncle Harvey has a new Plymouth. Went down to the woods & got some bittersweet. Played around with Richard. Got some corn & gourds. Made some cider.

Jackson School teenagers on a hayride made it into the *St. Paul Pioneer Press* in 1945.

Teens—mostly girls— danced at a North St. Paul canteen in about 1947. Nice bobby socks.

Weds. October 11. Went to school. Arthur Johnson and I went downtown and tried to sneak every show downtown. Got chased all around by a night watchman. Art got socked real hard by him. Got a couple of magazines.

Weds. December 6. Went to school today. Rode trucks after school. [Stole] some wine and drank it. After supper we hopped buses, trucks, street cars, and cars. We snuck in the Paramount Theater. We saw Marie Dressler in "Christopher Dean." It was swell.

At the top of the list of teen pleasures: sunning on a dock. These Girl Scouts were at camp in 1936.

Fri. December 8. Went to school. Got excused at one o'clock. Mildred Hitchcliff wrote my excuse. Boy! She sure is a honey.

Sat. December 16. Rode behind cars in the morning. Went to Montgomery Wards with Bob Jewell. In the afternoon we rode on a streetcar. The flatfeets [police] came along & caught Bob but I got away. Bob snitched on me. They caught Johnny & he snitched on Eugene Larson. I had to stay in all the rest of the day.

Sun. December 31. Last day of the year. Went to the Hamline Theater to see "The Bowery." I went to the theaters one hundred eleven times during this year. Went to three different schools this year. Got expelled from two of them. Had a couple girl friends. Margery Keeler was my favorite. My favorite occupations were studying birds, hopping freights and passengers & trucks. The greatest event of mine was when I attended the Worlds Fair in the last part of August. My favorite boy friends were Eugene Larson, Art Johnson, Russ Johnson & Bob Jewell & Erny Lundblad.

Romance

The most charming of all our recreations was a ride to "Little Falls," now "Minnehaha." The picture in my mind of this gem of beauty makes the sheet of water wider and more circular than it is now [in 1888]. I know it was fresher and newer, and there was no saloon there then, no fence, no tables and benches, cut up and disfigured with names and nonsense, no noisy railroad, no hotel, it was just our dear pure "Little Falls" with its graceful ferns, its bright flowers, its bird music and its lovely water-fall. And while we children rambled on the banks and gathered pretty fragrant things fresh from their Maker's hand, listening the while to sweet sounds in the air and to the joyous liquid music of the laughing water, there may have been some love-making [in the old-fashioned sense of courting] going on in the cozy nooks and corners on the hill side or under the green trees, for in later years I have now and then come upon groups of two, scattered here and there in those same places, who looked like lovers, which recalled to my mind vividly what I had seen there long ago.

Charlotte Ouisconsin Clark Van Cleve, 1820s–30s

One day a letter came from Smith Clary telling me that he was coming to Anoka to buy sash and doors for the house he was building for his mother. This was an excuse, he added. He was really coming to see me.

He brought with him a book for my mother entitled "Looking Toward Sunset." (Ma was then 45 years old.) He also presented me with "Farm Ballads" by Will Carleton (very popular at that time).

Smith spent several days with us, and during that time he hired a horse and buggy to take me riding. We went to a beautiful little lake. There he stopped the horse, and we viewed the scenery. Before we started for home, our future was arranged. When I reached the age of 20 and he 24, we were to be married.

The plan was Smith's. I had not thought of marriage except in a dim, distant future. My mother often said that 24 was the ideal age for a girl's marriage (the age of her own).

Don't imagine that our memorable ride was so free from romance as I have made it. When I go to a movie, I want to look away or shut my eyes on the love scenes. I am glad there was no candid camera about. Only the woods, the lake and the sky overhead witnessed our idyll.

Smith bought the sash and doors for his mother's house and said he would build a finer house for me. After he left, the wife of the owner of the sash and door mill (a woman we didn't know) told someone that a fine young man, visiting at the Methodist parsonage, had bought sash and doors for a house. She supposed Miss Lathrop was about to be married. Small-town gossip, I

Nothing like a good
smooch under a tree.
This one was delivered in
about 1910.

hear you say. Everyone, except intimates, thought me 18 or more. But I was
just past 16 and Smith a few weeks less than 20.

Nothing was said to my parents about an engagement. But when Smith
left, he kissed me good-bye in the presence of the family.

Anna Lathrop Clary, 1860s

*Wyman X. Folsom of Taylors Falls was seventeen was he was mustered into
the army during the Civil War. Fourteen months later, he wrote to his mother,
asking what she thought of his beloved.*

Saint Louis
Oct. 17, 1863

My Dear Mother,

I must write you a few lines letting you know I am well and in good spirits.
No, I am not in good spirits. I never was so homesick in my life as now. I
want to get out of this devilish army—am tired and sick of being cat-hauled

round. This good war is going to use up more men than can be replaced in 4,000 centuries . . .

Mother you asked me if Annie and me was engaged—what do you think about it—I want your advice, if you say so I will drop all with her. If I allways think as I do now I will marry her sometime. Now, mother, state your feelings plain to me about it, will you. If you say stop I will, even if it kills her, as for *me I can stomach anything.*

Mother did not approve. Wyman dropped Annie.

Nov. 25, 1863

I think you are right in regard to me and Annie. I am now satisfied she is not the one to make me a wife, and *what in the devil* do I want to think marrying now . . . I thank you for your good advice. I am now contented that you know more than I do.

* * *

May 23, 1863

Ross Nichols went to kiss Sallie Sibley, when she gave him a swat with her hand, which blooded his nose. A good deal of fun was created by the disappearance of Etta Ingersoll & Charley Curtice, and Martha and Charley Rittenhouse in the bushes, & on their reappearance the boys were greeted with hallos although nobody suspected them of doing anything out of the way.

"Until death (or teen years) do us part . . ." Young love at another mock wedding in 1948.

Feb. 19, 1864

We went over to Goodings [party] where we found a large crowd, and more coming in . . . There was the greatest set of girls there that I ever saw. About the toughest one was Eva Lyons, she would get someone to introduce the boys to her, and then she would grab them and kiss them! . . . I never saw such a party. After a while, I blew out the light. The kissing and smacking, till a light was brought in, sounded like a flour mill. There was a second of time in which not a dozen kisses were let off.

Frederick Allis

"Uncle Dudley" in 1882 offered an early version of Ann Landers's advice to the lovelorn.

Julia, You are in a pickle, sure enough. You say you gave your "adorable" the "mitten" [broke off the relationship] and now you are sorry you did so, and want us to tell you the best way to win him back without having to go through too much humiliation. Well, let us see. You had better write him a note, perfumed with sassafras and things, and tell him you were only joking—that you are just as much his as possible without the aid of a parson—that your heart is in his vest pocket, or in that vicinity, and he ought to know it. If this doesn't work, just write to him again that you are anxiously awaiting his reply to your last, before yielding to the persuasions of another chap, who is absolutely turning yellow for the want of your smiles. This will bring him, if he isn't a fiend, and if he is a fiend, it will be dead sure to fetch him.

*   *   *

Two teenage boys from Oakport Township, a few miles north of Moorhead, started a neighborhood newspaper in 1884. Walter Draper and one of the Probstfield boys were upset that local girls had started a paper and boasted of running male editors out into the cold.

The boys responded, "We intend to stop their gab by publishing a paper that will outshine them all. We do not intend to employ any females, or they would say we could not get a paper up without their help." They wanted to name their newspaper the Eclipser *or* Paralyzer, *but those names were already taken somewhere, so they chose* The Draper *and* Probstfield Monthly News. *An annual subscription was eight dollars—a lot of money then.*

Here's what Walter published, with his spelling intact, on October 25, 1884:

Young Ladies: I have been listning some time to the talk on "women's rights" and if you will "lend me your ears" I will says a few words. It is a subject in which I am interested, as I blive the ladies propose to remove King Alcohol from our land, behead him as it were. But fair girles, this is a power which is not within you reach and you may never have the opportunity to walk to the polls and vote side by side with the stern sex but you need not stand idly, waiting for something to do, but go to work at once. I have no doubt but that the ladies of our Lyceum would vote for Prohibition had they an opportunity. Yet in my experience and observation a great majority of them lend their influence in the opposite direction. I imgine I can see the brows of some of the fair girles darken at this, but it is true neverthless. Say for instance, if every young lady should decide, I will neither keep company with, nor marry a man who indulges in intoxiating liquors. Don't say if you take that stand that you would live and die an old maid. It is my opinion: far better to live in single blessedness than a life of doble cussedness.

PERSONAL—A young man, stranger in the city, desires the acquaintance of a respectable young lady, with matrimony in view. She must be handsome, have a heart "as good as gold," or if she has got some money or a good business, so much the better. Please address x43, Tribune.

Minneapolis Tribune, November 15, 1885

For the box social, each single girl prepared a supper for two and packed it in a box. She usually decorated it elaborately. The boxes were sold to the single men and boys at the social. The highest bidder became her supper partner. Bidders were not supposed to know which girl had packed the box. If a bidder was persistent in trying to get a certain box, his friends suspected that he knew it belonged to a girl he especially wanted as a supper partner. They enlivened the bidding for a while by modestly raising his bids.

Agnes Mary Kolshorn, about 1910

A little listener:
    Father—"What did you and John talk about last night?"
    Daughter—"We talked about our kith [friends] and kin [family]."
    Small brother—"Yeth, pop, I heard 'em. He said, 'Kin I have a kith,' and she said, 'Yeth, you kin.' "
"Oak Hill Topics," published by the young women of Mrs. Backus' School for Girls,

St. Paul, February 1917

Like most young girls with diaries, Coco Irvine recorded her love life.

Dear Diary,
This is to be my most private account of everything that happens to me.
    NO ONE MUST READ A WORD FURTHER UNDER PAIN OF DEATH. A CURSE SHALL BEFALL ANY WHO DISREGARD THIS WARNING.
    Everything is getting quite different in my life because of boys! I absolutely like one now. I guess he likes me too. This diary is to keep track of how

Coco Irvine at the age of thirteen, when she kept a diary recording her love life

things go. And so I can analyze the best way of making certain he likes me. He sure acts like he doesn't, which is a good sign.

Saturday, January 1, 1927
This boy I like goes to Sunday school. I have known him many years but never knew I really liked him til I started dancing school last fall.

Friday, January 6
Dancing School night. Hope he will be there!

Later—He was. He danced with everyone but me. That's a good sign because even tho he didn't dance with me, He looked at me three times. I had fun with [friend] Charlie.

I danced three times with Charles, six times with Bobby and four times with George and that's all. Only I don't like them too much and they are only valuable as people who can keep me from being stuck. I have to cultivate as many people as possible so that won't ever happen.

Friday, January 13

HE didn't dance with me til the very end. He said, "You seem to be awfully
clubby with Charlie." I said, "Well you never dance with me, so I have to
amuse myself somehow." He said, "Oh, but I save you for the last." I said, "Is
that a compliment?" He said, "You should know," but I still don't. A person
could take that as either yes or no. It is most *aggravating.*

Sunday, January 9

Last night I went skating at the University Club rink. *He* was there! I was
wearing my red jacket and cap. I was practicing my figure eights which I
don't know how to do very well when HE came skating up to me. He said,
"You look like Red Riding Hood and you know what happened to her." "The
wolf came and ate her all up," and he made a horrible face at me. "He'd have
to catch her first," I said, skating away nearly as fast as I could. He came
after me and of course caught me, being good at hockey. He grabbed me
around the waist and I thought he was going to kiss me and I tried to decide
whether to let him. He didn't though. He pushed me away and skated as fast
as anything around and round the rink. Showing off I guess. This was all
very romantic.

Sunday, January 15

We all went skating tonight and then back to my house. We played Truth
and Consequences and Winkum, both of which entail kissing. It can be fun
if you know how to do it right. In Winkum you have to look at a boy in a
certain way and then wink at someone else. This is aggravating to the first
boy who thinks you plan to let him kiss you. And a joyous surprise to the
person you wink at. I tried this on three boys and fear I made three friends
and three enemies. Maybe it isn't such a good idea. I winked at Charlie twice
(I owe it to him for the dancing with me and all) and once at *him. He* didn't
seem at all surprised. In Truth and Consequences I asked him who he liked
best of girls. He said he hated them all and what did I think of that? It was
11:30 P.M. before I got to bed. I was so tired.

January 27, 1927

My thirteenth birthday. I got a card [a disciplinary note from school],
but this is Friday and my birthday and dancing school night so just as I
suspected, mother, not being a fiend, let me go. She gave me a new dancing
school dress which is actually sleeveless. A great concession! Also it is not
pink or blue (like usual) but green taffeta. I look really old in it except for my
feet. She made me wear my same black patent leathers. She says high heels
are absolutely out because I would break my neck. [Brother] Tom gave me
a compact. [Sister] Lib sent a telegram and daddy gave me $10.00. A *very*
satisfactory day. At dancing school all the girls were pea-green with envy

Maud Knight and Gordon Coster in 1921 seemed to be stuck more on each other than on the Hans Brinker book. That's a rolling hoop, not a hula hoop of later generations.

and made derogatory remarks about sleeveless dresses. I was amused to see Dotty and Dede wore their dotted swisses! (Really childish.) Dede's even had a sash. Imagine! I had the best time. Everyone danced with me even Him, although he had to ruin it all by remarking, "Even I don't feel I can ignore you on your birthday." I don't know how I can stand him and told him so. He said, "Who's asking you to?" Ye Gods!

Summary of 1927
It is now New Years Eve of 1927. I have kept this diary for one whole year.

In looking back over this past year I feel I have become a great deal more mature. When I started this diary, I was but a child in many ways, though old for my age. There are many things I did earlier in the year that seem silly to me now. I still like HIM but it doesn't seem so important any more to find out if he likes me. I figure he must be a moron wasting so much time trying to exasperate me. Besides I can make him mad by ignoring him and making scathing remarks.

But of all things that happened this year, the most important was that someone [her older sister's boyfriend] thought me charming. I can't help but think so too.

A person who is charming surely shouldn't have to worry about Him any more.

Now I must get ready to go out for New Years Eve. We're all going over to the Archers and we plan to call our parents every 15 minutes all evening. They won't have time to have any fun at all.

Happy New Year, dear diary, I can't wait for 1928, can you?

Love

"Coco"

In Case You Were Wondering

Why did you research about children? They have been overlooked in history. And they have great stories to tell. Besides, each of us was a child once. How many topics have such wide appeal?

Why do people—even young children—look so stern in old photos? Two reasons: early photography required long exposures of very still subjects. Holding a pose for several seconds proved especially difficult for fidgety children. Sometimes props were used to keep the subject's head steady. Occasionally you can see a long metal rod behind a person's back for stability.

Also, making a photograph was a rare and momentous event until the late 1800s. Subjects felt they should look distinguished and wealthy, certainly not grinning sillily. Just as with notables who had their portraits painted, it was the custom to look somber. Even children. Now it's the opposite: photographers insist "Smile," even at a non-smiley moment.

Did lots of children keep diaries and write letters? Yes. It was fashionable in some circles, especially among the better educated before World War I. Not many of the children's documents survive. But neither will the text messages kids send today.

Were the "good old days" good for children? Not especially. Just as today, some kids had it made with loving family, generous parents, safe environments, and exciting adventures. But many had it rough. Violence, poverty, and neglect are nothing new. Read here about the orphan trains and young soldiers and children hanged for crime. Childhood—the age of innocence? Nope, not for many.

Where did you find all this stuff? I got to poke around in the collections of the Minnesota Historical Society, considered one of the nation's finest state historical organizations. I also looked in various county societies, some private collections, and other libraries. So can you. It's lots of fun. And free, almost. (You may have to pay a bit for copies.) Many historians and librarians love to share what they know and will help you find what you need. Or, if you wish, you can hire a professional to do the digging for you. Ask at your history center.

Why are the dates for so many photos in this book labeled "about" such-and-such a time? And why aren't all the people in the pictures named? That's because not all those who went before us took the effort to properly identify their photos. We should. Please do it for your family.

Why did you keep writers' odd spelling and vocabulary and sentence structure? I find them charming, and it helps me realize that kids who slaughter the written language today may turn out reasonably well anyway.

*Why do you have so much **old** stuff, and not much about more recent times?* C'mon, this is history: it's supposed to be old. But seriously, material from decades ago is more readily available. Odd, but true. For instance, Civil War information is voluminous, but little about the Iraq War, and even the Vietnam War, has made its way to history centers. Also, as time has passed, letter and journal writing has become less and less common.

Please consider donating your letters, diaries, or photos to your regional or state historical society so that researchers can someday effectively document the current years. Print out some special e-mails too, including ones from soldiers overseas.

Why are some groups and regions represented better than others? Some Minnesota counties have terrific history centers, and others, well, their holdings are paltry.

Members of dominant ethnic groups, such as the Scandinavians and Germans, did an exceptional job of saving materials and putting them into safe places. Other groups are underrepresented. African Americans and American Indians, for example, kept their records in different forms and relied heavily on oral stories. They had lost so many of their traditions and stories that they were understandably reluctant to hand over their history to mainstream repositories. Now such historical societies recognize the importance of diverse materials and are eager to learn from the records of a wide variety of people.

And finally, a question I hadn't expected but one that people frequently ask me: *Which Minnesota family had the most children?* Sorry: I don't know, and historians don't know how to help me find out. If you have a candidate for the honor of Minnesota's biggest family, please let me know.

But we need to remember that defining *family* isn't so easy. Just one set of parents? Blended families? Adopted and foster children? Children informally taken into a home?

Just as today, families of old were complicated.

Thanks

A huge thanks to all the people who helped me find photos, diaries, reminiscences, and jokes about childhood in Minnesota over the generations and to the many who helped me pull this book together. One very good thing about historians is they like to share their knowledge.

Here are some of their names, and I ask forgiveness of those I've missed:

Minnesota Historical Society librarians and archivists: Ruth Bauer Anderson, Tracey Baker, Patrick Coleman, Dave Ehasz, Debbie Miller, Steve Nielsen, Kathryn Otto, Alison Purgiel, Brigid Shields, Hampton Smith, and Duane Swanson.

Minnesota Historical Society specialists: Marcia Anderson, Linda Cameron, Dana Heimark, Brian Horrigan, Linda McShannock, Steve Osman, and Cheri Thies.

Minnesota Historical Society reference assistants: Carol Benik, Nick Duncan, Kristen Helgeson, Jennifer Huebscher, Eric Ondler, Will Peterson, and Noah Skogerboe.

Minnesota Historical Society Press staff: Ann Regan, editor in chief; the late Will Powers, production manager; Pam McClanahan, director; and Gregory Britton, former director.

Historians at other Minnesota historical societies: Kathy Evavold and Chris Schuelke of the Otter Tail County Historical Society; Char Henn, Johanna Grothe, and Diane Buganski of the Goodhue County Historical Society; Jack Kabrud and Susan Larson-Fleming of the Hennepin History Museum; Walter Bennick and Mark Peterson of the Winona County Historical Society; Patricia Maus of the Northeast Minnesota Historical Center, Duluth; Mark Piehl of the Historical and Cultural Society of Clay County; Linda Schloff and Susan Hoffman of the Jewish Historical Society of the Upper Midwest; the Aitkin County Historical Society, the Fillmore County Historical Society, and the Ramsey County Historical Society.

Other historians and researchers: Annette Atkins, history professor at Saint John's University, Collegeville; Sandy Date of the *Star Tribune* library; Scott D. McGinnis of Historical Research Services, Chaska; historian Barbara Sommer; Minneapolis Public Library librarians; and the Minnesota Historical Society's monthly research group.

Steadfast friends: Jane Curry, Carol Hartman, Kris Henn, Marilyn Hoegemeyer, Gretchen Kreuter, Rebecca Lindholm, and Ingrid Sundstrom Lundegaard.

My great appreciation goes to two fine historians: Debbie Miller of the Minnesota Historical Society, who knows that I love children, talked me into this project, and offered years of wisdom and support; and Shannon Pennefeather, my fine editor at the Minnesota Historical Society Press, whose intellect, enormous patience, and organizational skills helped shape this book.

Sources

Minnesota Historical Society, St. Paul, abbreviated as MHS
Some selections are identified with the excerpts.

A Little Taste

W. W. Clary Papers. "Reminiscences of Anna Lathrop Clary." MHS.

W. W. [Mr. Billy] Smith. Ann Smalley Jordan Archives. Otter Tail County Historical Society, Fergus Falls. Used with permission.

Blanche Stoddard Seely Papers. MHS.

Isabel Thibault. *My Island: Memories of a Childhood on Gales's Island.* Excelsior, MN: Excelsior–Lake Minnetonka Historical Society, 1978. Used with permission.

Glanville Smith Papers. Stearns History Museum, St. Cloud. Used with permission.

Clotilde Irvine. *Coco's Diary: The Diary of a 13 Year Old Girl, circa 1927.* West St. Paul: Olivia Irvine Dodge, 1975.

Lydia Samuelson. In *Aitkin County Heritage.* Aitkin, MN: Aitkin County Historical Society, 1991. Used with permission.

Governor Floyd B. Olson Papers. MHS.

Nancy Perry Hawkins Letters. MHS.

Charlotte Blizen Papers. "Through Charlotte's Eyes." Jewish Historical Society of the Upper Midwest, Minneapolis. Used with permission.

Home Life

Birth

Lena Borchardt Papers. MHS.

Abby Weed Grey and Family Papers. Note and "Oak Hill Topics." MHS.

Ruth F. Brin. *Bittersweet Berries: Growing Up Jewish in Minnesota.* Duluth: Holy Cow Press, 1999. Used with permission from Judith Brin Ingber.

Sandra Kreamer. *A Menu of Memories: A Jewish Family's Stories and Recipes.* Edina, MN: Beaver's Pond Press, 1998. Used with permission from Sandra Winer.

Parenting

Samuel W. Pond. *The Dakota or Sioux in Minnesota as They Were in 1834.* St. Paul: MHS Press, 1986.

John Henry Mitchell and Family Papers. MHS.

Walter Stone Pardee Papers. Hennepin History Museum, Minneapolis.

M. C. Russell. *Uncle Dudley's Odd Hours: Western Sketches, Indian Trail Echoes, Straws of Humor.* Lake City, MN: Home Printery, 1904.

Robert D. Hill Papers. MHS.

William M. Cummings Papers. MHS.

Evelyn Fairbanks. *The Days of Rondo.* St. Paul: MHS Press, 1990.

Siblings
W. W. Clary Papers. "Reminiscences of Anna Lathrop Clary." MHS.

Walter Stone Pardee Papers. Hennepin History Museum, Minneapolis.

Names
Warren Upham. *Minnesota Place Names: A Geographical Encyclopedia.* 3rd ed. St. Paul: MHS Press, 2001.

Charles Eastman. *Indian Boyhood.* 1902. Reprint, New York: Dover Publications, 1971.

Governor Floyd B. Olson Papers. MHS.

Coming to Minnesota
Maude Baumann Arney. Papers and journal. MHS.

Fannie S. Schanfield. "Ma, I Wrote It Down." Jewish Historical Society of the Upper Midwest, Minneapolis. Used with permission.

Carl Warmington. *Living a Full Life During the 20th Century: An Autobiography.* Bradenton, FL: The author, 1999.

Homes
Walter F. Benjamin Papers. MHS.

Edmund Rice Papers. Writings by Maria Rice Dawson. MHS.

Blanche Stoddard Seely Papers. MHS.

Margaret Jackson Bovey Papers. MHS.

Robert M. Shaw. *A Minnesota Lumberjack in France, 1917–1918: The World War I Diary of Robert C. Shaw.* [Minnesota]: The author, 1987.

Animals
W. W. Clary Papers. "Reminiscences of Anna Lathrop Clary." MHS.

Charles Eastman. *Indian Boyhood.* 1902. Reprint, New York: Dover Publications, 1971.

Lena Borchardt Papers. MHS.

Maude Baumann Arney. Papers and journal. MHS.

Agnes Mary Kolshorn Family History. MHS.

Isabel Thibault Papers. MHS.

Nellie Stone Johnson. *Nellie Stone Johnson: The Life of an Activist.* [As told to] David Brauer. St. Paul: Ruminator Books, 2000.

Betty Powell Skoog. *A Life in Two Worlds.* With Justine Kerfoot. Lake Nebagamon, WI: Paper Moon Publishing, 1996.

Shirley Schoonover. "Route 1, Box 111, Aurora." In *Growing Up in Minnesota: Ten Writers Remember Their Childhoods,* edited by Chester G. Anderson. Minneapolis: University of Minnesota Press, 1976, pp. 153–54. Used with permission.

Challenges

Social Agencies
Minneapolis Humane Society Records. MHS.

"Little Stories about Little Sisters." Special collections, Minneapolis Public Library. Courtesy of the Hennepin County Library, Kittleson World War II Collection.

Big Brothers Annual Meeting, 1950. Special collections, Minneapolis Public Library. Courtesy of the Hennepin County Library, Minneapolis Collection, M2714.

Orphans

Rev. Hastings H. Hart. "Placing Out Children in the West" (pamphlet). MHS.
Public Welfare Department Records. MHS.
Evelyn Fairbanks. *The Days of Rondo.* St. Paul: MHS Press, 1990.

Crime

Alice Mendenhall George. *The Story of My Childhood, Written for My Children.* Whittier,
    CA: [W. A. Smith], 1923.
Northfield Bank Robbery Papers. MHS.
Ramsey County Probation Department Papers. Y-Gang Club Leaders Diaries. State
    Archives. MHS.

Seasons

Summer

Blanche Nichols Wilson. *Minnetonka Story: A Series of Stories Covering Lake
    Minnetonka's Years from Canoe to Cruiser.* Minneapolis: Colwell Press, 1950.
Frederick L. Johnson. *The* Sea Wing *Disaster.* Red Wing, MN: Goodhue County Historical
    Society, 1990.
Lena Borchardt Papers. MHS.
Margaret Jackson Bovey Papers. MHS.
Melvin Lynn Frank. "In North Minneapolis: Sawmill City Boyhood." *Minnesota History*
    47.4 (Winter 1980): 141–53.
Gerhard A. Ellestad. *Small Town Stuff.* [Minnesota]: The author, 1985.
Manuel Ruder. Interview by Linda Schloff. Jewish Historical Society of the Upper
    Midwest, Minneapolis. Used with permission.
Lawrence Schaub. "Drought and Dust." In Their Words: Stories of Minnesota's Greatest
    Generation. MHS. Used with permission.
Evelyn Fairbanks. *The Days of Rondo.* St. Paul: MHS Press, 1990.
Sandra Kreamer. *A Menu of Memories: A Jewish Family's Stories and Recipes.* Edina, MN:
    Beaver's Pond Press, 1998. Used with permission from Sandra Winer.
William Albert Allard. *Time at the Lake: A Minnesota Album.* Duluth: Pfeifer-Hamilton
    Publishers, 1998.

Autumn

Frederick Allis. Diary and additional materials. Courtesy his great-granddaughter, Betsy
    Allis, Minneapolis.
Lena Borchardt Papers. MHS.
William M. Cummings Papers. MHS.

Winter

Charlotte Ouisconsin Van Cleve. *"Three Score Years and Ten": Life-long Memories of Fort
    Snelling, Minnesota, and Other Parts of the West.* 3rd ed. Minneapolis: Harrison and
    Smith, 1895.
W. W. Clary Papers. "Reminiscences of Anna Lathrop Clary." MHS.
Walter F. Benjamin Papers. MHS.
Blanche Stoddard Seely Papers. MHS.
Melvin Lynn Frank. "In North Minneapolis: Sawmill City Boyhood." *Minnesota History*
    47.4 (Winter 1980): 141–53.
Charlotte Blizen Papers. "Through Charlotte's Eyes." Jewish Historical Society of the
    Upper Midwest, Minneapolis. Used with permission.

Dorothy Snell (Tenenbaum) Curtis. "Dreams on Ice." In Their Words: Stories of Minnesota's Greatest Generation. MHS. Used with permission.

Timothy Trent Blade. "The 1940s Remembered in the 1980s." *Hennepin County History* 48.2 (Spring 1989): 20–27.

Maude McGuire Papers. MHS.

Spring

Polly Bullard. "Remembrance of Things Past: The Reminiscences and Diary of Polly Caroline Bullard." MHS.

Glanville Smith Papers. Stearns History Museum, St. Cloud. Used with permission.

Games and Toys

Charlotte Ouisconsin Van Cleve. *"Three Score Years and Ten": Life-long Memories of Fort Snelling, Minnesota, and Other Parts of the West.* 3rd ed. Minneapolis: Harrison and Smith, 1895.

Frederick Allis. Diary and additional materials. Courtesy his great-granddaughter, Betsy Allis, Minneapolis.

Charles Eastman. *Indian Boyhood.* 1902. Reprint, New York: Dover Publications, 1971.

W. W. Clary Papers. "Reminiscences of Anna Lathrop Clary." MHS.

P. O. Tilderquist Family Papers. MHS.

Alexander Ramsey Papers. MHS

Polly Bullard. "Remembrance of Things Past: The Reminiscences and Diary of Polly Caroline Bullard." MHS.

Evelyn Fairbanks. *The Days of Rondo.* St. Paul: MHS Press, 1990.

Marietta Neumann. "Stories of Farm Childhood in the 1930s." Share Your Story Project. MHS. Used with permission.

V. Lynette McKewin Kimble. "Family Life in the 1930s." Share Your Story Project. MHS. Used with permission.

Blade, Timothy Trent. "The 1940s Remembered in the 1980s." *Hennepin County History* 48.2 (Spring 1989): 20–27.

Movies

Gerhard A. Ellestad. *Small Town Stuff.* [Minnesota]: The author, 1985.

Robert Williams McKewin. "Going to the Movies." Share Your Story Project. MHS. Used with permission.

Celebrations

Birthdays

W. W. Clary Papers. "Reminiscences of Anna Lathrop Clary." MHS.

Clarrissa Blandin Stebbins Papers. MHS. Used with permission.

Alexander Ramsey Papers. MHS

Glanville Smith Papers. Stearns History Museum, St. Cloud. Used with permission.

Ruth Marion Skoglund. Diary. Permanent collection. Goodhue County Historical Society, Red Wing. Used with permission.

William M. Cummings Papers. MHS.

Holidays

Ruth Marion Skoglund. Diary. Permanent collection. Goodhue County Historical Society, Red Wing. Used with permission.

Frederick Allis. Diary and additional materials. Courtesy his great-granddaughter, Betsy Allis, Minneapolis.

Lillian MacGregor Shaw. *Wonder Woman!: Lillian MacGregor Shaw, Age 96, Talks About Her Early Years.* As told to Robert MacGregor Shaw. [Minnesota]: R. M. Shaw, 1987.

Larry S. Greenstein. "The Pumpkin Man." Share Your Story Project. MHS. Used with permission.

W. H. C. Folsom and Family Papers. MHS.

W. W. Clary Papers. "Reminiscences of Anna Lathrop Clary." MHS.

Alice Mendenhall George. *The Story of My Childhood, Written for My Children.* Whittier, CA: [W. A. Smith], 1923.

Walter Stone Pardee Papers. Hennepin History Museum, Minneapolis.

Andrew Swanson Papers. Writings by Annie Swanson Gaslin. MHS.

Marjorie L. Bullard Papers. MHS.

Emily Panushka Erickson. "Growing Up in St. Paul: West Seventh Street: Czechs, Slovaks, Bohemians, and Kolache Dough Rising in the Warm Attic." *Ramsey County History* 32.2 (Summer 1997): 22–26. Copyright © Ramsey County Historical Society. Used with permission.

Food

Charles Eastman. *Indian Boyhood.* 1902. Reprint, New York: Dover Publications, 1971.

Frederick Allis. Diary and additional materials. Courtesy his great-granddaughter, Betsy Allis, Minneapolis.

Fannie S. Schanfield. "Ma, I Wrote It Down." Jewish Historical Society of the Upper Midwest, Minneapolis. Used with permission.

Blanche Stoddard Seely Papers. MHS.

Lillian MacGregor Shaw. *Wonder Woman!: Lillian MacGregor Shaw, Age 96, Talks About Her Early Years.* As told to Robert MacGregor Shaw. [Minnesota]: R. M. Shaw, 1987.

Evelyn Fairbanks. *The Days of Rondo.* St. Paul: MHS Press, 1990.

Sandra Kreamer. *A Menu of Memories: A Jewish Family's Stories and Recipes.* Edina, MN: Beaver's Pond Press, 1998. Used with permission from Sandra Winer.

Historic Events

Civil and Dakota Wars

Bircher, William. *A Drummer-Boy's Diary: Comprising Four Years of Service with the Second Regiment Minnesota Veteran Volunteers, 1861 to 1865.* Edited by Newell L. Chester. St. Cloud: North Star Press, 1995. Used with permission.

Mary Newson. "Memories of Fort Snelling in Civil War Days." *Minnesota History* 15 (1934): 395–404.

Marion Ramsey Furness. "Childhood Recollections of Old St. Paul." *Minnesota History* 29 (June 1948): 114–29.

Depression

Rodney Howard Duncan. "My Memories Through the 30s, 40s and 50s." Share Your Story Project. MHS. Used with permission.

V. Lynette McKewin Kimble. "Family Life in the 1930s." Share Your Story Project. MHS. Used with permission.

Governor Floyd B. Olson Papers. MHS.

World War II

Ruth Feser Hale. "Home Front Memories." Share Your Story Project. MHS. Used with permission.

Dorothy J. Pederson Nelson. "Teenage Memories of the Home Front." Share Your Story Project. MHS. Used with permission.

Joyce A. (Bosak) Meyer. "Child at War." Share Your Story Project. MHS. Used with permission.

Well-Being

Health

Isaac Grant Haycraft Papers. MHS.

Lillian MacGregor Shaw. *Wonder Woman!: Lillian MacGregor Shaw, Age 96, Talks About Her Early Years.* As told to Robert MacGregor Shaw. [Minnesota]: R. M. Shaw, 1987.

Alexander Ramsey Papers. MHS

Jo Lutz Rollins Papers. MHS.

Lena Borchardt Papers. MHS.

Emily Panushka Erickson. "Growing Up in St. Paul: West Seventh Street: Czechs, Slovaks, Bohemians, and Kolache Dough Rising in the Warm Attic." *Ramsey County History* 32.2 (Summer 1997): 22–26. Copyright © Ramsey County Historical Society. Used with permission.

Glanville Smith Papers. Stearns History Museum, St. Cloud. Used with permission.

Irene Krumpelmann Papers. MHS.

The Moccasin (July 1939 and August 1942). Ah-gwah-ching, MN: Minnesota State Sanatorium.

Elizabeth Kenny Papers. MHS.

Death

Alexander Ramsey Papers. MHS

Frederick Allis. Diary and additional materials. Courtesy his great-granddaughter, Betsy Allis, Minneapolis.

Lewis Johnson. Diary. Permanent collection. Goodhue County Historical Society, Red Wing. Used with permission.

P. O. Tilderquist Family Papers. MHS.

Margaret Jackson Bovey Papers. MHS.

Holbeck family history courtesy Historical and Cultural Society of Clay County.

Stickney letter in Abby Weed Grey and Family Papers. MHS.

J. C. "Buzz" Ryan. *Tall Timber.* Duluth, MN: St. Louis County Historical Society, 1982. Used with permission.

Walter Stone Pardee Papers. Hennepin History Museum, Minneapolis.

Irene Krumpelmann Papers. MHS.

Learning

Education

Harold H. Pond. "Edward Robert Pond and Mary Frances Hopkins." Minnesota Chapter Pond Family Association of America, 1954.

Frederick Allis. Diary and additional materials. Courtesy his great-granddaughter, Betsy Allis, Minneapolis.

Charles Eastman. *Indian Boyhood.* 1902. Reprint, New York: Dover Publications, 1971.

Alexander Ramsey Papers. MHS

Bruce Weir Benidt. *The Library Book: Centennial History of the Minneapolis Public Library.* Minneapolis: The library, 1984.

Karl Raymond in "Book of Remembrance." Archives. Westminster Presbyterian Church, Minneapolis. Used with permission.

Alma Scott Papers. MHS.

J. C. "Buzz" Ryan. *Tall Timber.* Duluth, MN: St. Louis County Historical Society, 1982. Used with permission.

Fannie S. Schanfield. "Ma, I Wrote It Down." Jewish Historical Society of the Upper Midwest, Minneapolis. Used with permission.

Ruth F. Brin. *Bittersweet Berries: Growing Up Jewish in Minnesota.* Duluth: Holy Cow Press, 1999. Used with permission from Judith Brin Ingber.

The Moccasin (July 1939 and August 1942). Ah-gwah-ching, MN: Minnesota State Sanatorium.

Indian Boarding Schools

Brenda J. Child. *Boarding School Seasons: American Indian Families, 1900–1940.* Lincoln: University of Nebraska Press, 1998.

John Rogers. *Red World and White: Memories of a Chippewa Boyhood.* Norman: University of Oklahoma Press, 1996.

Manners

Lydia Maria Francis Child. *The Mother's Book.* Boston: Carter and Hendee, 1831.

Walter Stone Pardee Papers. Hennepin History Museum, Minneapolis.

Harvey Green. *The Light of the Home: An Intimate View of the Lives of Women in Victorian America.* New York: Pantheon Books, 1983.

Alexander Ramsey Papers. MHS

Thomas Edie Hill. *Hill's Manual of Social and Business Forms.* Chicago: W. B. Conkey Co., 1901.

Lillian MacGregor Shaw. *Wonder Woman!: Lillian MacGregor Shaw, Age 96, Talks About Her Early Years.* As told to Robert MacGregor Shaw. [Minnesota]: R. M. Shaw, 1987.

Frederick Hunt Letters. MHS.

Marion Levitan Kaplan Gebner. "Saying It Like It Is." Jewish Historical Society of the Upper Midwest, Minneapolis. Used with permission.

Music

Edmund F. Ely and Family Papers. Catherine Ely diary. Northeast Minnesota Historical Center, Duluth.

Lewis Johnson. Diary. Permanent collection. Goodhue County Historical Society, Red Wing. Used with permission.

Iva Andrus Dingwall Papers. MHS.

Blanche Stoddard Seely Papers. MHS.

Margaret Jackson Bovey Papers. MHS.

Glanville Smith Papers. Stearns History Museum, St. Cloud. Used with permission.

Reuben Berman. "A North Minneapolis Childhood." *Hennepin History* 56.1 (Winter 1997): 22–35.

Carl Warmington. *Living a Full Life During the 20th Century: An Autobiography.* Bradenton, FL: The author, 1999.

"Hit Singles," "80 Years of American Song Hits," and "Variety Music Cavalcade." Minneapolis Public Library.

Growing Up

Fashion

Samuel W. Pond. *The Dakota or Sioux in Minnesota as They Were in 1834.* St. Paul: MHS Press, 1986.

Alice Mendenhall George. *The Story of My Childhood, Written for My Children.* Whittier, CA: [W. A. Smith], 1923.

Blanche Stoddard Seely Papers. MHS.

Jo Lutz Rollins Papers. MHS.

Lena Borchardt Papers. MHS.

Melvin Lynn Frank. "In North Minneapolis: Sawmill City Boyhood." *Minnesota History* 47.4 (Winter 1980): 141–53.

Teri Ferguson Thompson. *As I Remember: Lakeside Reflections of Mary Gilson Ferguson.* Edina, MN: Beaver's Pond Press, 2002. Used with permission

Evelyn Fairbanks. *The Days of Rondo.* St. Paul: MHS Press, 1990.

Marietta Neumann. "Stories of Farm Childhood in the 1930s." Share Your Story Project. MHS. Used with permission.

Inventions

Charlotte Ouisconsin Van Cleve. *"Three Score Years and Ten": Life-long Memories of Fort Snelling, Minnesota, and Other Parts of the West.* 3rd ed. Minneapolis: Harrison and Smith, 1895.

Walter Stone Pardee Papers. Hennepin History Museum, Minneapolis.

Isaac Grant Haycraft Papers. MHS.

Charles Eastman. *Indian Boyhood.* 1902. Reprint, New York: Dover Publications, 1971.

Blanche Stoddard Seely Papers. MHS.

Lincoln H. Fey Papers. MHS.

Jo Lutz Rollins Papers. MHS.

Gerhard A. Ellestad. *Small Town Stuff.* [Minnesota]: The author, 1985.

Reuben Berman. "A North Minneapolis Childhood." *Hennepin History* 56.1 (Winter 1997): 22–35.

Morris Freedland Papers. Jewish Historical Society of the Upper Midwest, Minneapolis. Used with permission.

Jobs

Walter Stone Pardee Papers. Hennepin History Museum, Minneapolis.

W. E. B. DuBois. *Darkwater: Voices from Within the Veil.* New York: Harcourt, Brace and Howe, 1920.

J. C. "Buzz" Ryan. *Tall Timber.* Duluth, MN: St. Louis County Historical Society, 1982. Used with permission.

Gerhard A. Ellestad. *Small Town Stuff.* [Minnesota]: The author, 1985.

Nellie Stone Johnson. *Nellie Stone Johnson: The Life of an Activist.* [As told to] David Brauer. St. Paul: Ruminator Books, 2000.

Betty Powell Skoog. *A Life in Two Worlds.* With Justine Kerfoot. Lake Nebagamon, WI: Paper Moon Publishing, 1996.

Teens

Stickney letter in Abby Weed Grey and Family Papers. MHS.

Charles A. Lindbergh Papers. MHS.

William M. Cummings Papers. MHS.

Romance

Charlotte Ouisconsin Van Cleve. *"Three Score Years and Ten": Life-long Memories of Fort Snelling, Minnesota, and Other Parts of the West.* 3rd ed. Minneapolis: Harrison and Smith, 1895.

W. W. Clary Papers. "Reminiscences of Anna Lathrop Clary." MHS.

W. H. C. Folsom and Family Papers. MHS.

Frederick Allis. Diary and additional materials. Courtesy his great-granddaughter, Betsy Allis, Minneapolis.

M. C. Russell. *Uncle Dudley's Odd Hours: Western Sketches, Indian Trail Echoes, Straws of Humor.* Lake City, MN: Home Printery, 1904.

Walter Draper Manuscripts. Courtesy Historical and Cultural Society of Clay County, Moorhead.

Agnes Mary Kolshorn Family History. MHS.

Abby Weed Grey and Family Papers. Note and "Oak Hill Topics." MHS.

Clotilde Irvine. *Coco's Diary: The Diary of a 13 Year Old Girl, circa 1927.* West St. Paul: Olivia Irvine Dodge, 1975.

Index

Waiting for a Snow Day has been designed and set in type by Christopher Kuntze. The typefaces are Warnock Pro for the text, Adobe Birch for display, and Magma for the captions. The book was printed and bound by Sheridan Books, Inc., Ann Arbor, Michigan.